Robert Wringham is a writer and performer who lives in Glasgow and Montreal. He's the editor of *New Escapologist*, a small-press magazine for working stiffs with escape on the brain. The magazine, now in its tenth issue, has seen contributions from Alain de Botton, Richard Herring, Ewan Morrison, Tom Hodgkinson, Leo Babauta, Luke Rhinehart and other prominent citizens in support of the good life.

Wringham's first book, *You Are Nothing*, was published in 2012 by Go Faster Stripe and is a history of Dadaesque comedy troupe Cluub Zarathustra featuring Stewart Lee, Roger Mann and Simon Munnery. As a performer he does stand-up comedy, spoken word and performance art in places like the Traverse Theatre in Edinburgh, Mainline Theatre in Montreal, at the Edinburgh Fringe, the Montreal Infringement Festival, and the Glasgow CCA. As a humourist and essayist, he's written for the *Idler*, *Playboy*, *HiLoBrow*, the *British Comedy Guide*, *Splitsider* and a hundred other magazines and websites. As a humourist he writes about the minutiae of modern life, and as an "Escapologist" he writes about the larger mechanisms of the same modern life. A devastating wealth of his ridiculous stuff can be found at wringham.co.uk.

# ESCAPE EVERYTHING!

## ROBERT WRINGHAM

unbound

This edition first published in 2016

Unbound

6th Floor  Mutual House  70 Conduit Street  London  W1S 2GF

www.unbound.co.uk

Typesetting by Bracketpress

A CIP record for this book is available from the British Library

ISBN 978-1-78352-133-3 (trade hbk)
ISBN 978-1-78352-171-5 (ebook)
ISBN 978-1-78352-134-0 (limited edition)

Printed in Great Britain
by Clays Ltd, St Ives Plc.

9 8 7 6 5 4 3 2 1

For Samara

All my mind is filled with a single thought: to get free!
Get free! And the intoxication of that freedom,
that success, is sublime.
— Houdini

Dear Reader,

The book you are holding came about in a rather different way to most others. It was funded directly by readers through a new website: Unbound. Unbound is the creation of three writers. We started the company because we believed there had to be a better deal for both writers and readers. On the Unbound website, authors share the ideas for the books they want to write directly with readers. If enough of you support the book by pledging for it in advance, we produce a beautifully bound special subscribers' edition and distribute a regular edition and e-book wherever books are sold, in shops and online.

This new way of publishing is actually a very old idea (Samuel Johnson funded his dictionary this way). We're just using the internet to build each writer a network of patrons. Here, at the back of this book, you'll find the names of all the people who made it happen.

Publishing in this way means readers are no longer just passive consumers of the books they buy, and authors are free to write the books they really want. They get a much fairer return too – half the profits their books generate, rather than a tiny percentage of the cover price.

If you're not yet a subscriber, we hope that you'll want to join our publishing revolution and have your name listed in one of our books in the future. To get you started, here is a £5 discount on your first pledge. Just visit unbound.com, make your pledge and type thedailygrind in the promo code box when you check out.

Thank you for your support,

Dan, Justin and John
Founders, Unbound

# FOREWORD

## by DAVID CAIN

Every time I write a piece advocating escape from corporate servitude, I receive a few emails that contain a particular kind of scolding. They tell me that only an entitled brat could be dissatisfied with a stable job and a roof when so many pine for only these things.

If that's the case, then we live in a world built of, and for, legions of such entitled brats, whether they choose to actually implement their escape plan, or only think about it all day. For all the financial prosperity of the modern world, there's a certain poverty in our willingness to take pay to perform activities that have, typically, almost nothing to do with our personal values. As if there were no better ideas out there, we take up this yoke by the thousand, slotting ourselves into grids of grey squares, stacked 50 to a 100 high, sealed with a shiny glass exterior.

Even while the internet and its emerging cultures continue to hint at new modes of working and living, you may still be told it's *vain* to insist on a station more fulfilling than a permanent stall in a well-reputed grid. According to my critics, even if you find your standard weekday boring, painful or unfulfilling, you ought to embrace it, simply because a third-world coal miner would kill for your benefits package. When so many have so little, attempting to *escape* a situation in which you can reliably feed yourself and fund a retirement, could only be an act of the utmost ingratitude.

A minority of us believe the opposite is true: that escaping from an unfulfilling mainstream lifestyle isn't a moral failing, but rather a moral imperative. It's precisely *because* we have the necessary freedoms at our fingertips (and because others don't) that spending our lives in the stable isn't just foolish, but wrong. To remain, voluntarily, in a life where your talents are wasted and your weekdays are obstacles, is to be humble in all the wrong ways.

Robert Wringham, along with *New Escapologist's* readers and contributors, has come to represent to me this sensible minority. If you're reading this book, it's nearly certain that you're living with levels of *potential* freedom that nearly all of history's humans would envy, and that alone is reason enough to feel uneasy if you haven't yet made good on this gift.

The desire to escape corporate policy, consumer debt, meaningless work, or any other life-draining first-world cultural norm is not a symptom of greed. Rather, it's a reaction to a truth we don't like to talk about in the office: that, given our options, we're probably not using our lives very well. There may be, in any given tract of cubicles, that rare round peg, whose values exactly match those outlined in his company's policy manual and mission statement, and for whom his years truly are best spent doing what his underboss would like him to do. But the truth is that most of us – simply by following the path prescribed by our schools, bosses and peers – end up entrenched in a set of roles that do not serve our deepest values and which, in the early hours of any given Monday, we do not especially look forward to fulfilling.

Still, we're liable to feel ambivalence whenever we think about deviating from norms of any kind. This affliction, which we might call 'rebel's doubt', may put us in danger of taking seriously the charges of selfishness and insularity we get from those who embrace the mainstream. 'Check your privilege!' they sneer, with latte in hand.

But with a bit of thought we can see that the failure of empathy is on their side. As our impoverished coal miner knows, only a fool would submit to living a single day as a peon when he has the means to escape in his back pocket. Limiting your freedom in some kind of token solidarity with the truly oppressed is like avoiding exceptional health simply because the chronically ill can't have it. I'm convinced now that a calculated escape from the status quo is an aspiration to a particular kind of health, which is only now beginning to catch on: a thoughtful, prosperous alignment of your values and your lifestyle.

In a world where such a thing is possible, you might think we'd all be trying on lifestyles until we found one that fitted. But relatively few do. As it stands, the norm is to pick a popular one, perhaps fully aware that The Man himself is at the helm, and run with it for several decades, even well after its ultimate irrelevance and emptiness begin to show. Meanwhile, we complain fondly about it, make knowing jokes with our colleagues about it, steal pens and toner to reclaim some of our lost self-esteem, and if we're lucky, become at least numb to the work itself. What makes it seem worthwhile is that the proceeds allow us to build, in our evenings and on weekends, a fraction of the life we wanted all along.

Why is this kind of needless languishing still such a dominant tradition? At least partly, it's because we're told from childhood the celebrated lie that quitters never win. Again, only a little thought is necessary in order to see the holes here: condemning egress in general implies that *nothing* should ever be abandoned once it's entered, whether it's a deadening career, a dead relationship, or for that matter, a burning building.

Using *New Escapologist* as a lens, Robert has shown us the enormous misuse of human energy that is this status quo, as well as what can flourish in ordinary people when that energy is reclaimed and repurposed. Human beings, it turns out, are most prone to creating original and valuable things when they *haven't* auctioned off their prime daylight hours to rich speculators. *New Escapologist* gives us the community – and vocabulary – with which to explore that notion and start to recover some of that long-lost value.

It's a discussion that is by its nature irreverent, and often hilarious. If we're talking about how to escape the tyranny of The Man, we eventually encounter other pressing questions. How can I carry both my office and wardrobe in a 28-litre backpack? Is a beard a worthwhile project for a young man in the twenty-first century? Is putting both lemon and sweetener into your tea a ghastly lapse of decency, or is it moral progress? Escaping the bonds of conventional living frees one to focus on such topics with impunity.

Zooming out, Escapology is a witty but ultimately serious examination of that ancient philosophical question – *how should we live?* – but applied this time to the modern world, where it's normal to be already living out someone else's answer by the time the question even occurs to you.

You're about to begin, if you haven't already, a one-way trip into The Good Life – this kind of wisdom is irreversible, after all – and Mr Wringham is the perfect guide.

David Cain
Escapee

# INTRODUCTION:
# THE LITTLE MAN CHALLENGED

*Stone walls do not a prison make, nor iron bars a cage.*
— Richard Lovelace

've seen behind the curtain. It was horrible. But it was all right too. I was a bored twenty-something when I got my glimpse. I'd taken an interest in the history of conjuring. That is, stage magic. This didn't come entirely out of nowhere – I wanted to be a comedian and found myself thinking about stagecraft and the more unusual flavours of it – but it was still unlike anything I'd read before. Magic history was fusty, mischievous, Victorian, sequinned, inconsistent. It felt like privileged information, even though the books I'd read were simply from the public library. For a while, the Indian rope trick, 'Pepper's Ghost', and mysterious characters like 'Long Tack Sam' and 'The Great Wizard of the North' really did it for me. I had reproduction posters of Houdini and Kellar on the walls of my rented apartment, the stains left by the Blu-Tac eventually claiming 50 quid of my security deposit.

Concerning myself with the history of conjuring – at a time I was supposed to be starting a career of some sort or, at least, coming to terms with the street value of a 2:1 psychology degree from the University of Wolverhampton – probably wasn't what is commonly considered useful. Magic makes you think in a logical but also mischievous way: exactly the way you're *not* supposed to think when you've a long career of network administration and photocopier unjamming ahead of you. It makes you want to know what lies hidden behind certain curtains.

Ultimately, it was Houdini who tipped me off. Or perhaps it was somehow the effect of returning to a day job on Monday mornings after a weekend with century-old magic. Like the bends, it was a sudden and severe change in pressure. Perhaps this clanging together of atmospheres – the white-collar and the sensational – caused something to shatter and momentarily reveal an exciting and terrible truth. However it happened, I saw it, and some things – a dog's bollocks, a fat man trying to pick up a watermelon seed – can never be unseen.

The truth is: we're caught in a trap. All of us. We're a society of largely decent but completely unknowing *Wind in the Willows* types, cast asunder in a gigantic juicing mechanism. Elements of modern life we've come to see as normal – going to work, going shopping, farting about on Twitter, feeling inexplicably but consistently blue – are all parts of The Trap. The Trap keeps us comfortable enough and may even extend our lifespans, but only for as long as we're content to stay inside it, all the while being juiced and *digested*. You might have known about this already – there are clues everywhere – and perhaps you're happy to go along with it, in which case carry on. On the other hand, this could be news to you and you might like to join me in an act of escape.

'Welcome aboard,' said the young recruitment officer. He theatrically opened a door to reveal the bank of warmly humming computers for which I was now responsible, as if to say 'all of this is yours'. But I didn't want it to be mine. I didn't care about computers, warmly humming or otherwise. I wanted to do something titillating and in line with my new-found mystical interests. I lacked the patience to be a magician, but if I applied myself I could be a witty writer like Myles na gCopaleen, or a great comedian like Simon Munnery, or a transvestite potter like Grayson Perry.

Egotistical perhaps. Dreamy certainly. But Jesus Christ, look at the alternatives. Network Administrator. Outreach Officer. Teaching Assistant. *Forever*? With *my* remarkable mind and half-decent singing voice? Not bloody likely. I didn't want to eat machine-vended sandwiches for lunch in the staff canteen of a concrete carbuncle, listening to co-workers bicker about who used up the milk. I wanted a rider in my sumptuous dressing room, overflowing with exotic fruit and the undies of groupies. What's wrong with that?

I'm not an employee by nature. Nobody is. On the other hand, if I was unable to cover the rent this month I'd be out on my arse. Hence this job. I was trapped. Trapped, potentially, for the next 40 years, which at the age of 23 really does look like forever. The jail time for bank robbery is nowhere near that long. I know because I checked. *Welcome aboard...*

I heard the hum of the computers. I smelled the static electricity coming off them. A rarely used LED on the control desk in my brain suddenly lit up. It was the one marked 'escape'. Grayson Perry and the others couldn't help me now. Of all my heroes, only Houdini could get out of this one.

It really was Harry Houdini who showed me the truth behind the curtain. Could we, like he from his boxes, escape the biggest trap of all? Houdini – himself no stranger to exotic fruit and the undies of groupies – was 'the handcuff king', able to free himself from the cuffs of any challenger as well as jail cells, packing crates, mail sacks, and straitjackets. On a particularly beguiling evening, he even escaped the rotting carcass of a whale. 'Nothing on Earth can hold Houdini a prisoner,' boasted his posters. To this day, we best know him as the Master Escapologist. Chances are, you once named a hamster after him.

Some of Houdini's most bewitching feats, though, weren't escape-based at all. As a magician he made coins dance enchantingly between his fingers, caught bullets between his teeth, and made an elephant called Lulu vanish into thin air. Making Lulu disappear remains one of the greatest magical accomplishments ever, perhaps one of the most impressive theatrical performances if judged by sheer spectacle. To this day, nobody quite knows how Houdini did it. He was a prominent and controversy-courting sceptic, the Richard Dawkins of his day – but less embarrassing to bring up at parties. He was a movie star, an author, a pioneer aviator, an agent of the US Secret Service, the star of his own Broadway show. He was, as his most recent biographers call him, the first American superhero. But he was most famous – and still is – for picking locks.

When you stop to think about it, an escape act is a very odd piece of theatre. What could be entertaining about watching someone spend painstaking minutes – even hours – picking a lock or wrestling his way out of a box? It's even odder when you learn the audience didn't actually *see* those things at all. If Houdini were to escape a packing crate, the very nature of the performance rendered both him and his process completely obscured from view: the audience who paid to see Houdini escape spent much of their time in the theatre gawping at a wooden box. String quartets were hired to keep the audience interested while he struggled inside the crate. To escape a set of handcuffs, Houdini would retreat mysteriously behind his 'ghost box', a canvas screen designed to obscure his process. Even if you'd been able see the performer there would not have been much to see. There was no sensational 'trick' and certainly no real magic. Houdini picked locks. That's what happened behind the screen. A vanishing elephant or a bullet caught between the teeth is a clearly witnessed feat with a tantalisingly mysterious technique. But this? This was a man in a box. A hundred urbanites in a poorly ventilated room, eyes fixed upon a slightly wobbling crate sounds like a very odd piece of fringe theatre, but it was in fact an international sensation.

Escapology – above other forms of magical entertainment – must have struck a chord in the collective consciousness. He must have tapped something deeper than the desire to be entertained. Houdini's work, writes the psychoanalyst Adam Phillips, 'was essentially the devising of ever more unusual, exacting, and marketable tricks that would, in an unwitting way, exploit and expose the habits of the country'. Could it be that Houdini's act transcended mere spectacle and stepped into the world of metaphor? Through a popular entertainment and the engineering of absurd situations, he 'exposed the habits of the country' and so, in his way, was a satirist. 'It wasn't really conjuring at all,' writes magic historian Jim Steinmeyer, 'even if his novel act had been derived from the world of magicians … The drama … was the sight of the little man challenged, playing David to society's endless Goliaths, the archetypal victim who, within the strict confines of the vaudeville turn, rose to be the victor.'

The 1900s, when Houdini was at the height of his popularity, provided many such Goliaths. It was a time of profound social and technological change. Edison's phonograph made a cheap and portable commodity of music; Ransom Eli Olds began producing the first ever marketable cars; it was a time of colonial expansion; nations of erstwhile farmhands were coming to terms with bureaucracies and corporations; advertising had begun to reframe conveniences as essentials. It was the start of what we currently know as the consumer economy.

The average person was fairly helpless in the face of this relentless progress, and so Houdini acted on his behalf – symbolically – by picking the locks of handcuffs, bursting from wooden crates, and even finding his way out of a police van designed to transport criminals. *'The little man challenged,'* Steinmeyer said. If it were possible to escape such physical shackles, would it not also be possible to escape the socially constructed ones that bound millions of normal people to modern lives of alternating consumption and toil? After all, social shackles aren't even really there. They're not forged from iron in the fires of Birmingham like the ones Houdini mocked. I believe it was this flirtation with possibility that made Escapology so appealing.

Houdini's performances were metaphors, pantomimes of the cultural escape fantasy. He represented emancipation: liberation from traps being set by the unseen architects of the new economy. His devout scepticism – his public reputation for debunking spiritualists, many of whom were powerful politicians and celebrities – suggested that not every institutionalised commandment need be obeyed. And if magic could be held in the benign hands of a formerly poor rabbi's son and one-time locksmith's apprentice, maybe it could be held by anyone. Houdini, without an overt agenda, drew attention to the new predicament of industrialised nations: that it's a trap and that traps can be escaped.

Whizz forward a hundred years to the early twenty-first century. Look out of the window, look into your hearts. We still identify with 'the little man challenged'. We're still in The Trap. It's the self-same trap set in Houdini's day but it's now more effective than ever before. Most people born in The Trap are unaware of its existence let alone that they're in it. The consumer economy and a nominal democracy have led to improvements in quality of life but also to new affronts to liberty. Meaningless jobs and massive debts, for example.

As many as 80 per cent of us are dissatisfied with our jobs. We spend an intolerable number of hours working and further unpaid hours in trains and buses and traffic jams getting to and from work. Despite these sacrifices, most of us are in debt because we're so desperate to reclaim our dignity as consumers. In Canada – one of the most efficient industrialised nations of them all – the average citizen ended 2013 in with a non-mortgage debt of $28,853. Already we can see The Trap in action. We work to pay debts, we accrue debts because of the indignities of work.

Once you subtract work, shopping and sleep, there isn't much time left for freedom. When are we to have real fun? When are we to better ourselves? When are we to read and oversleep and cook and make love? Why must these activities be pushed into 'spare time', into the margins of life when they could be the substance of it? Marginalising fun and fretting over debt can't have been what people had in mind when they set out to build a civilisation. Escaping this situation, as individuals and as societies, is the subject of this book.

We should apply Houdini's magic to real life. The modern world needs Escapology. We need the lock picks, the patience, the knowledge and humour to escape the manacles and jail cells. We need to know how to leave jobs we don't like, to ignore the siren song of consumption, to escape debt, stress, bureaucracy, and marketing. We need to know how to escape the imprisoning mindsets that come with the consumer economy: miserliness, background unhappiness, passive-aggression, *mauvaise foi*, competitiveness, and submission.

Seeing the solution as Escapology leads us to think about it in a particular way: not only that any trap can be escaped, but also that it can be escaped with a kind of aplomb, a sense of fun, playfulness and challenge. Just as Houdini accepted a public challenge each time he performed and gradually picked the lock so that he might find freedom, we can do the same. I challenge *you*, dear reader, to escape whatever manacle restrains you. Bad relationship? Escapology! Horrible job? Escapology! Ingrowing toenails? Escapology! But also a chiropodist.

Why not become a modern-day Escapologist? Study each trap carefully with Houdini's scientific eye, and break free. In 2007, a year or so after my initial interest in the history of magic and a year after taking that rubbish office job, I set up a magazine called *New Escapologist*. It asked whether the magic of Escapology could be brought down to the rest of us. Is escape from The Trap possible? If so, how might we arrange it? Can we *all* escape or do we need someone to stay inside The Trap to keep pulling the levers and turning the cranks? Just as I'd hoped, *New Escapologist* acted as a beacon and I was soon talking to and working with hundreds of other people enthusiastic about the arts of everyday escape. It gave me a vantage point from which I could see even further behind that curtain. Now I can tell you that escape *is* possible. Quickly and radically or slowly and carefully, escape is possible. Treat with suspicion the people who tell you it's not.

# PART ONE

# THE TRAP

## IN WHICH WE WEIGH UP OUR PREDICAMENT

Here follows a long description of a machine.
— Houdini

# WORK

I think that in a year I may retire. I cannot take my money
with me when I die and I wish to enjoy it,
with my family, while I live.
— Houdini

## MY FIRST JOB

*rump, crump, crump.* The virgin snow gave way beneath each
footfall. For four years, whenever it snowed, mine would be
the first footprints around our neighbourhood. They went up
the big hill and down again, continuing in and out of a hundred different driveways.

People didn't want the newspaper I was delivering. It wasn't a proper
one like the *Guardian* or the *Times* that they'd paid for and expected,
but a weekly free paper called the *Dudley News* that was filled mostly
with advertising and non-stories about 'local tots'. If you made the
mistake of reading the *Dudley News* or handling it in any way or even
looking at it too closely, you'd come away plastered with cheap, dirty
ink. I was occasionally chased off people's doorsteps for trying to deliver their paper or perhaps because, all inky, I looked like a Dickensian
scoundrel. Looking back, I can't imagine why I didn't just dump the lot
in a recycling bin at the start of each round, since that's where they were
destined to go within an hour of delivery anyway.

What got me through the weekly paper round, I think, was a tell-
ingly consistent hope that a bored housewife might flash me from a

bedroom window like something from a Timothy Lea *Confessions* movie. My only defence is that I was 14 years old and I was growing up in the West Midlands and watching a lot of Timothy Lea *Confessions* movies. Naturally, the only things I saw through windows while delivering newspapers were my school friends watching cartoons in cosy living rooms, while I was inevitably being snowed on or pelted by hailstones and trespassing in their driveway.

I continued with this little job for three years because it seemed to make my parents happy (they admire hard work) and because I quite liked getting paid. And, lest we forget, because I imagined there was an ever-so-slight chance of seeing some boobs. The other fantasy I carried around in addition to the newspapers was that when I grew up, I'd have a more dignified and meaningful and interesting job than a paper round. Alas, by the time I had an office job, my chance of seeing boobs in the workplace had decreased from slim to none and I had marginally less purchasing power. Bugger.

## AN OUTLANDISH COMMITMENT

'So let me get this straight,' no one ever says, 'You want me to commute to a place, remain there for eight hours while doing things I don't particularly want to do in the company of people I don't particularly like, and to do so for five days out of seven for about 40 years? Are you out of your tiny *mind*?' After all, who would do that? It turns out, almost everyone. As journalist Ellen Goodman once put it: 'normal is getting dressed in clothes that you buy for work, driving through traffic in a car that you are still paying for, in order to get to a job that you need so you can pay for the clothes, car and the house that you leave empty all day in order to afford to live in it.'

There aren't enough people saying '*How* many hours?' and 'Until *what* age?' and 'You're pulling my fucking *leg*'. We typically work 40 hours a week. Some people work longer – as in the scandalous case of low-paid bankers' interns in London – and some people are lucky or unlucky enough, depending on their circumstances, to work fewer. But 40 hours is typical. This figure does not account for the undeclared hours put in by enthusiastic go-getters or for the time lost to the 'always on' culture promoted by mobile technology. Today you can be effectively at work when you're on a hot date or having a poo.

Forty hours a week, for forty years of your life is a breathtaking commitment. Even if you happen to be a professional chocolate-taster or a watcher of exciting movies, 40 years of your life is quite an expectation. We reluctantly spend 87,000 hours at work before retiring or dying (and it's optimistic to assume that the former will happen before the latter). We also spend 5,000 hours commuting to and from work. I couldn't find a survey to suggest how many hours we spend preparing for work and recovering from work, but it must be a mind-bogglingly hideous number. When you work full time, every vacation, weekend, bank holiday, nightly sleep and stolen moment is but a recovery from work. We don't occupy those moments in their own right any more: we use them to recover from work. 'How was Christmas?' you might ask a colleague. 'Oh, it was just nice to be off,' she'll say. Under such circumstances, home is no longer home but a kind of docking station or pit stop to facilitate more work. Christmas is no longer about midwinter merriment but a temporary hiding place from the boss.

And then there are the dreams! The dreaded work dreams. I once had a Saturday job in a large branch of W. H. Smith. I'd sometimes have prolonged and embarrassingly dull dreams about collecting abandoned shopping baskets from around the shop. This was a real part of my job, so repetitive a task that it must have burrowed its way into my unconscious mind. When I woke up, it occurred to me that I'd worked a shift that I couldn't possibly be paid for. This does not seem to be an uncommon experience and work dreams are all too often work *anxiety* dreams. We experience so much stress and frustration in our jobs and such separation anxiety from our non-work projects, that it affects our sleep. Is this really worth it? Should my boss have made me feel so anxious about collecting up the abandoned shopping baskets that I'd end up dreaming about it? Unfortunately, there's not much we can do about this unpaid invasion of our most private respite until some kind of ethereal dream currency is instated as a pay cheque for hours worked during a dream or until, of course, we engineer less anxiety-producing circumstances to enjoy when we're awake. Abolish work, I say! Get rid of it! Or at least make it pleasant enough not to disturb our sleep and ruin our lovely dreams.

Here's the Dalai Lama's sweet phrasing of the problem: '[modern man] sacrifices his health in order to make money. Then he sacrifices money to recuperate his health. And then he is so anxious about the future that he does not enjoy the present; the result being that he does not live in the present or the future; he lives as if he is never going to die, and then dies having never really lived.'

## WHY WORK IF WE HATE IT?

In 2014, a courtroom stenographer had spent around 30 trials typing the words 'I hate my job' over and over. It was properly hilarious and caused a minor internet sensation. Journalist Dawn Foster wrote of it, 'the fact that so many people gleefully shared this story shows that many of us, deep down, harbour a suspicion that our jobs aren't necessarily what we want to be doing for the rest of our lives' and 'For some bizarre reason, it's still taboo to admit that most jobs are unspeakably dull'.

Some people like their jobs and that's excellent. Just because I've never enjoyed a job, it does not defy belief that there might be good ones out there: well paid, altruistic, satisfying jobs with daily variations and the opportunity to do something worthwhile and well. There are also stories of saintly hospital porters or bus drivers who win the lottery and say 'I won't let it change me though' and continue to go off to work each morning a secret millionaire. It makes you wonder why they bought a lottery ticket in the first place, but more power to them. For the vast majority, however, work is not enjoyable and is at best a nuisance. 'The daily grind', we call it, or 'the rat race' or 'the salt mine' or 'the sweat shop'. There aren't any positive colloquialisms for the act of going to work. There aren't any Irish folk songs or American blues ballads about how the singer loves his boss and his work is fulfilling and the bankers are doing a super job of managing his perfectly reasonable earnings.

Nobody, when they were eight, wanted to grow up to be a server in a fast food franchise or a quantity surveyor or, God forbid, a 'co-director of digital innovation'. They may have wanted the benefits of such jobs – to be wealthy or to wear an exciting hat – but only a weirdo would fantasise about the attendant duties: being stuck in the same place five days out of the week, doing the same brain-liquefying tasks over and over again for quite spurious reasons.

There are many reasons to have a job. Normality is one: we work because other people work and have done since as far back as we can remember. It would be outrageous not to join in. There's also the obedience element. An experiment described by Stanley Milgram in 1963 showed how regular people are capable of quite extreme behaviour (administering what they thought were electric shocks to a frail old man) just because someone in a lab coat prompted them to do so. The laboratory door was open throughout and the participants were told at the beginning that they could quit at any time, yet they'd continue at the simple suggestion of 'please continue' or 'the experiment requires that you continue'. Most people will continue in a destructive or pointless task at the gentlest suggestion from authority. The real-life 'suggestion' that we buck up our ideas and get a job is not so subtle, and it's very hard to disobey it.

We do not go to work because we enjoy it or because it is noble to do so. We go to work because we don't know any different, because authority requires it of us, and because – the primary reason – we must earn a living. Moreover, we must earn a living because we live in a society in which to do otherwise would result in poverty. Hour by hour, pay cheque by pay cheque. A job is a short-term solution to a long-term problem.

'Work is the source of nearly all the misery in the world,' writes anarchist Bob Black. 'Almost all the evil you'd care to name comes from working or from living in a world designed for work. In order to stop suffering, we have to stop working.' Bob Black is right. In his words, we should end employment, support the right to be lazy, favour full unemployment, and agitate for permanent revelry. The Surrealists said something similar but 'unlike the Surrealists,' says Bob Black, 'I'm serious'.

So am I. The alternative is not outright laziness (though there's nothing especially wrong with that) but a more creative, deliberate and beneficial form of activity. Anyone who's enjoyed luxurious indolence – perhaps an extended sick leave, or time spent comfortably on a redundancy payment – will know there comes a time when you want to get up off your arse and act: the body and mind did not evolve to lie in bed forever. But the will to act after such a leisurely period will be deliberate, self-initiated and, above all, consensual: there will be no storm trooper prodding at you to go to work like there is now. Consent, incidentally, is the keystone of our current moral system. Consent is what informs our laws, our democracy, our social relationships and attitudes to sex. Work, when we remember that it's not quite a consensual act since we have little choice but to go along with it, is lagging behind in terms of the moral norms in our society. This is why it ought to be abolished or at least radically reconsidered.

The conversion of unemployment benefits into 'Jobseeker's Allowance' in the UK – the optimistic idea being that nobody is truly unemployed but on temporary hiatus from work and actively seeking more of it – ensures there's absolutely no choice but to work. This lack of choice is why work is sometimes referred to as wage slavery. We might not like it, but unless we do something unorthodox, we're completely dependent upon a wage. This unorthodox act – the escape from work – should preoccupy any self-respecting Escapologist. Work is a costly and not-entirely-consensual commitment. Those of us with bigger ideas or more pleasant designs on life want out!

## BULLSHIT JOBS AND INSPECTING INSPECTORS

There's a lot to dislike about work, especially today. Most of the time, all that makes it necessary is our need for money. Much of the actual labour and reporting for duty is superfluous. As Buckminster Fuller put it, 'we've got inspectors of inspectors and people making instruments for inspectors to inspect inspectors.' He's right. There are entire swathes of government in existence solely to keep people employed. I've had jobs that existed simply because someone else in the office was good at raising funds and had found the money from somewhere to pay for a new staff member, for whom there wasn't a real project or remit. I once asked colleagues in a hospital library if they'd consider a well-paid job digging a hole in the morning and filling it up again in the afternoon. They agreed they'd do it and that it wouldn't be so different from what they do in real life. 'Don't knock it,' said one, implying that my job with them was equally futile. It was.

There are real jobs out there – firefighters, doctors, nurses – but it's easier for a job-creating society dependent on maximum employment to generate less-skilled jobs that almost any nincompoop can do. It's also more tempting as an individual to accept a pointless job since becoming a firefighter or a doctor or a nurse would involve properly hard work and would expose us to danger, poopoo and guttywuts more often than we'd like. This was almost certainly my own reasoning on leaving school: it seemed the easiest option to quickly get onto a career path to inconsequential, white-collar mediocrity or face the horror of the poopoo. Alas, my squeamish, self-centred seventeen-year-old self had yet to encounter true boredom, understand how corrosive it could be to the soul or how little it meant to the world in terms of personal sacrifice or contribution. Escapology is perhaps the preserve and saviour of those in pointless jobs. Those prepared to face the full horror of life, death and bodily fluids may not need it. The tendency toward pointless jobs means we too often end up as functionaries in machines that should have either wound down years ago or never have existed in the first place. 'We keep inventing jobs,' said Buckminster Fuller, 'because of this false idea that everybody has to be employed at some kind of drudgery because, according to Malthusian-Darwinian theory, he must justify his right to exist' and rightly concludes 'we must do away with the absolutely specious notion that everybody has to earn a living.'

Jobs are sometimes the result of spin. After a scandal or costly mistake appearing in the newspapers, a big company or, more common-ly, the government, want to be seen to take action. So they 'launch an investigation' and set up a new department to begin making amends for whatever went wrong – supposedly assuring it won't happen again. This is inefficient and results in work that doesn't really need to be done. Over the course of the twentieth century, observes David Graeber in a now-famous essay called *On the Phenomenon of Bullshit Jobs*, the number of workers employed in industry, in farming or as domestic servants has 'collapsed dramatically'. At the same time there has been a tripling of people employed in 'professional, managerial, clerical, sales and service' positions, growing 'from one-quarter to three-quarters of total employment'. That's a lot of activity happening for the simple purpose of people needing money to live on. Is there really no better way of allowing people to live?

As time moves on, more and more people are doing pointless work. They might as well be getting paid for hopping around on pogo sticks or repeatedly opening and closing a desk drawer or copying out the Yellow Pages. Frankly, as journalist Tim Kreider puts it, 'if your job wasn't performed by a cat or a boa constrictor in a Richard Scarry book, I'm not sure I believe it's necessary.' Properly productive jobs have either been outsourced to countries with poorer or less-unionised populations than the UK and US; are now done by robots or computers; or have been eliminated where our social wants have changed. What we're left with in the West are white-collar or service jobs existing largely to keep people employed, to prop up the economy, to provide income for richer people and to sell junk nobody needs. We've become obsessed with work for the sake of itself. This has endangered the humanity it's supposed to serve. Still, at least work's a good place to get free Post-it notes and Blu-Tack for your vintage magic show posters. A small compensation for a life of mindless submission.

Even the remaining meaningful, socially worthwhile jobs are weighed down by bullshit tasks. Nurses, social workers, allied health professionals, librarians, teachers, surgeons, firefighters: all must tackle the bullshitberg of form filling and 'continued professional development' and fire drills and lip service. It creeps in through health and safety; the over-professionalisation of the human desire to help or care; funding justification; a personal or industry-wide fear of becoming obsolete; and a personal or departmental fear of not looking busy or white-collar.

As a society, could we change this? The absurd injustice of it makes me want to rail against The Trap and campaign for mass change, not just to escape The Trap but to jigger it, once and for all, from within. Such a campaign would be more than a full-time job though, and

I'm not the martyr type: I choose Escapology over utopianism. It's something I can do by myself.

Our best hope, as a society, for getting rid of it is to budget for and adopt a Citizen's Income. Citizen's Income is a guaranteed sum of money, given by the State, to every citizen. It would be enough to fund our basic subsistence needs. In other words, the government would give each of us something in the region of £75 per week: just about enough to live on. By giving this basic income to every citizen – regardless of age, physical ability, education, or wealth – we'd abolish poverty and make work less essential. Most people would still want to work in order to increase their quality of life, but it would be a choice rather than, as it currently stands, an unpleasant obligation. Frugal Escapologists could afford to discount work altogether; people who'd like to work part-time would be better equipped to do so; risk-averse people who'd like to start a business or become artists would finally have a safety net allowing them to do so; and – so long as housing remains affordable in relation to Citizen's Income – nobody would have to go hungry or sleep in a shop doorway again. Bullshit jobs, since nobody would need work for work's sake, could fall to the wayside.

Since everyone, regardless of their circumstances, would be in receipt of Citizen's Income, nobody would be made to feel like a scrounger or a freeloader or the recipient of charity. We'd be less obliged to tolerate unpleasant working environments since we'd be better empowered to walk away from them. We could spend our unemployed time doing useful or pleasant things for ourselves or for society instead of flipping patties in fast food outlets or watching the red hand of the office clock tick away our days. It would make shelter an inalienable human right. At last, the prevailing culture of our society would serve liberty instead of restrict it.

It would be funded by consumption taxes on luxury goods; green taxes on corporations who use or contaminate our shared natural resources; modest tax increases in the working population; and by savings incurred by dismantling the expensive bureaucratic systems that maintain and police the existing welfare systems. It has been questioned, rightly, whether we'd have enough tax revenue when everyone is working less. As well as the economic report we commissioned for Issue 9 of *New Escapologist*, some more serious economic institutions seem to think we would. Having said so, the most vocal champions of Citizen's Income in recent years, the Green Party of England and Wales, dropped CI as its flagship economic policy ahead of the 2015 General Election when the numbers could not be crunched accurately enough to win over a sceptical public. We'd need to get the tax sum right before embarking on such an ambitious scheme, but it's worth investing in the research to figure this out when one considers the ramifications.

It may sound idealistic but the idea has notable supporters from the political Left and Right alike. Pilots have been conducted in Germany, Norway and Canada, there's much public discussion about it in Switzerland, and it's one of the key policies of the Green parties of the UK. To keep appraised of opportunities to join a campaign to support Citizen's Income, keep an eye on the website citizensincome.org. Do your best to support a campaign whenever you become aware of one. It really could save all of our skins.

We *could* banish bullshit if we wanted to. But if the hostility towards the Green Party's Citizen's Income policy is anything to go by, the majority *don't* want to. Perhaps this is because not everyone has the temperament to live with the full glorious horror of freedom. Where we want freedom from The Trap, the only way to guarantee results is to go it alone. That's why it's Escapology and not utopianism. Utopianism, to a single person, is tantamount to terraforming: it can't be done without tremendous collective resource. As long as the majority aren't on side, we can either go along with the flow and dedicate ourselves to a job (perhaps even a meaningful, non-bullshit one like nursing if we can face the poopoo and guttywuts) or become Escapologists. The Escapologist must tool up (and for that matter tool *down* to be light on her feet) and meet the challenge and resistance to lone-wolfing with good humour. It might be lonely, but it's an accessible state and an actionable change we can make as individuals without needing to restructure society by banishing bullshit jobs.

## RADIUS OF ACTION
## AND KINKY RESTRICTION

A particular problem with work is that it usually keeps you tied to a certain place, restricting your freedom in that way. I have a friend who used to fly helicopters for the Canadian military. He told me about something called a *radius of action*: the distance an aircraft can travel in any direction before it must return to base for refuelling. If a chopper can hold enough fuel for 300 miles, its *radius of action* is 150 miles (150 out, 150 back): the 151-mile point being known as the *point of no return*. When we have jobs, we have a very small radius of action: we can only venture so far in our so-called free time before we must turn back for the next shift. A lunch hour provides a 30-minute radius of action, the 31st minute being a metaphorical point of no return. On a larger scale, an office worker can't very well go to New York on a whim if she must be back at a desk in London in 40 hours' time. Employees hit the point of no return very quickly and have to head back to the airport before they've had so much as a chance to ogle the Empire State Building or digest a single slice of pizza.

Having a job is like being tied to an elastic cord. You can stretch the cord for a while to get a sense of your environment but you'll always boing back to where you're apparently supposed to be. You're tethered, matey. This restriction in roaming rights is, for me, one of the worst things about work. Is it not an imposition that we're forced to report to a particular place at a particular time? Why does it not occur to us that this is a shocking restriction, one that runs absolutely contrary to our supposed treasuring of liberty? Elsewhere, placing such restrictions on one's radius of action is employed as a punishment: minor offenders being allowed to roam freely so long as they check in at a predetermined time and place. When your motions are dictated in this way, just as the growth of a sapling tree is dictated by the ties of a horticulturalist, we're all too often moulded into submissive little workers. It's masochistic. There's something deeply kinky in the way employers and management convert people into willing slaves. Unfortunately, this mass domination isn't an entertaining bit of fluffy-handcuff role play (though there *is* a safe word: 'sick day') since most of us don't really consent to take part and do so only because our livelihoods seem to depend on it. In the face of the remote working opportunities now available and the presentee-ism statistics published by the Office for National Statistics, the insist-ence that we work at a predetermined time and place for a requisite number of hours – no matter what needs doing or how efficient we might be at doing it – seems more and more absurd and unjustifiable. Teleworking could free whole swathes of employees from this kind of obedience: as long as we remain relatively accessible by email or Skype and complete the tasks required, who cares where and when we do them? Why don't we adopt these simple technologies wholesale? It can only be because productivity and liberty in our culture are secondary to commitment and obedience. Presenteeism meanwhile is when we show up at work even when we're unwell or incapable of working in some way or simply have nothing useful to do, because presence is either decreed by a contact or heavily suggested by a team-working culture. The fact that there's a name for this shows it's a known phenomenon, but still nobody's really trying to get rid of it. Work, the thing so many of us use to define ourselves, becomes an absurdist game of *Touch the Truck* (remember that?).

# HOW THE WEST WAS WON
# (BY WORK)

The way we work in the West today is not normal. We're so close to the world of work that we can't see what it's turned us into. Thankfully, a stroll through history can correct our perspective. Through the ages, work has been seen variously as a necessary evil, a form of play, a means of survival and a tedious duty to foist off onto slaves. I mention these modalities not to approve or disapprove of them but simply to offer a sense of perspective – to help show that the way we work today is not necessarily normal, right, or unchangeable. It's only quite recently we've started to see jobs as a way to distinguish ourselves. Slaves in Rome didn't sit around wittering about careers or job satisfaction, nor did medieval monks. In this regard, we live in a fairly unique period of history. For much of human time, the question 'what do you do?' would not have been a valid way to make chitchat at parties.

For centuries, humans lived as hunter-gatherers, living on wild fruits and the meat of wild animals. Hunting, gathering, eating, romping, art production and sleeping it all off were the main ways in which we were 'employed'. There was a strict one-to-one ratio of labour to wages: the wages of capturing a rabbit were precisely one rabbit and the wages of picking a handful of berries were, curiously enough, a handful of berries. It's unlikely that anyone defined themselves as hunter-gatherers since pretty much everyone did the same thing and, since there was no way to store the results of one's labour for any long period of time, people would have been unlikely to save or invest anything or to even value any material thing for the long-term. The notion of free time or a work-life balance did not exist: plenty of free time wasn't seen as a perk of the hunter-gatherer lifestyle but simply the natural state. There are still societies – the indigenous peoples of the Kalahari region of Africa and the Spinifex of Western Australia – who operate along these lines but they run into trouble with governments whose disdain for their lack of a fixed address makes them difficult to administrate.

In ancient Greece and Rome, most work was considered menial and undignified and not worth the attention of proper citizens. War, politics, business and philosophy were just about the only pursuits considered worthy of civilised people. While Aristotle praised agrarian ideals and the nobility of farmers, the farmers he had in mind were usually business people while the actual soil tilling was done by slaves. In fact, almost all real work was delegated to slaves because labour was considered arduous, trivial and a distraction from the good life. A citizen's duty was to cultivate ideals of a strong body and an active mind. Work was even seen a curse in the ancient world: the myth of Prometheus told that the theft of fire from the gods was punished by eternal toil for all men. The ancients did, of course, find a loophole in this curse and organised themselves according to a caste system so that at least some of them could avoid graft. Even slaves could eventually buy or earn their freedom through finding money or through courting their masters' affections.

The idea of work as a curse persists through early Christianity, 'the curse of Adam' (work) allegedly being man's share of the punishment for the eating of the forbidden fruit in the Garden of Eden. In medieval England, the Benedictine monks, however, began to see work as a form of physical prayer in as much as the maintenance of an abbey was a service to God. So long as it didn't detract from more traditional prayer, humble work was seen as having dignity. Moneylending and the accumulation of wealth were generally not encouraged – usury being explicitly frowned upon in the Bible – and work was not an end in itself: it was simply a way of facilitating the spiritual pursuits.

In the Renaissance, some forms of work were seen as positively noble but there was still a distinction between intellectual and menial work: architects and labourers. While the ancients had believed in the cultivation of body and mind, the people of the Renaissance also valued the cultivated, or trained, hand. Having multiple trades was something to aspire to, even if many of the attendant duties of such trades were, once again, seen as undignified and were outsourced to slaves. Artists like Botticelli had their own workshops and were seen as the masters of many creative disciplines, but they did not do all of the work themselves. While having ideas and finding ways to execute them had the glamour of genius, labouring was still menial and curse-like, and even painting was often delegated to skilled slaves.

The sixteenth and seventeenth centuries saw the Protestant Reformation and one of the most profound changes to the way work was seen in the Western world. We are still, today, in thrall to the Protestant Work Ethic. Theologians Martin Luther and John Calvin decreed that work was virtuous. Far from a curse bestowed upon humanity, it was in fact, a calling and an obligation. We must work because it is virtuous to do so, work being a direct commandment from God. Through work, they said, we would find identity, spirituality and something like self-worth. This is the origin of defining yourself through work. It is also the origin of earning a living as a kind of social obligation: where previous versions of Christianity (as well as Buddhism and Islam) had seen charity or the giving of alms as a spiritually-rewarding, even saintly action, Calvinism saw begging as freeloading and discouraged the act of charity. Money, said Calvin, should be saved and certainly not spent on anything as vain as charity, beautiful clothes, or feasts or festivals. Luther was against social mobility and working-class revolt, writing an influential essay charmingly called *Against the Murderous, Thieving Hordes of Peasants*.

The work ethic travelled across the Atlantic with the Puritans, and was secularised somewhat by Ben Franklin who believed in prudence, justice, thrift and hard work. It was eventually communicated efficiently through the Confederate States via children's stories, fables and improving literature: the dignity of hard work is still prevalent in American literature today. As late as the early nineteenth century, it was seen by optimistic Americans that employment was a temporary stop-gap before setting up shop for oneself, staking a land claim or starting a business. Until the mid-nineteenth century this was a fairly realistic prospect, but industrialisation soon took away this possibility: to create the kind of workforce necessary for industry, it was not in the interests of industrialists to allow self-sufficiency to continue as a valid prospect.

Industrialisation tamed the authority, devalued the skills and ultimately reduced the ideal of the craftsman to a romantic, perhaps even ridiculous, figure and hence radically changed the meaning of work. From here on, work was *employment* with the assistance of efficient mechanisation. It was no mean feat on behalf of the industrialists and people like Calvin to all but destroy the appetite for liberty and to promote the value of employed work in its own right. The effects of this effort were far-reaching.

Today, we still live in a culture defined by the Protestant Work Ethic. Secularisation and industrialisation may have reinforced it. We don't even have the idea of a religious calling any more, so we're not even working on the myth of a rewarding afterlife or a place in the spiritual elite. All we do is work to maximise our consumption privileges and to be able to tell people at parties that we're a lawyer, an artist or a police officer.

Sadly, though we lust after meaning and identity in our work, much of the labour that could be seen as tangibly useful has been exported to slaves once again (in the form of poorly paid workers in Asia) or is done by machines and computers. What remains is the 'bullshit job' – tweeting and marketing and supporting and supervising – and attempts at altruism through charitable or health sector work, which is constantly made difficult and unpleasant by the bullshit jobbers. The arts may offer some respite, but it is a flooded sector and is also dogged by a need for artists to also be skilled bullshitters in order to either market or justify their own products through 'artist statements' and funding applications and web presence. Almost everything is geared toward an

economic imperative – to make money – and our conservative governments and right-wing media are doing their best to dismantle the last
remaining opportunities for inherently good work: social institutions
like the NHS and the BBC in Britain. They want those institutions
rubbed out and replaced with private, moneymaking, debt-generating
companies.

By the 1960s, people began to worry about the alienation caused
by work. Industrialisation had uprooted people, deskilled jobs, discon-
nected people from their families and community life. A counterculture led by the hippies began to question the work ethic, which they
saw as repressive. In the 1990s, people felt betrayed by industrialisation:
Douglas Coupland's 1991 novel, *Generation X*, and *The Idler* magazine
pointed out that work divorced from craft and independence was a
stultifying bore. Big companies were downsizing, laying off huge
numbers of capable workers: Michael Moore wrote a high-profile book
about it called *Downsize This!* and a companion documentary film
called *The Big One*. The idea of loyalty to a company became a joke, for
loyalty is meant to be a reciprocal arrangement and nobody could trust
their employer to employ them into old age even with a contract.
Employees started to notice that their wages had begun to stagnate –
usually in the name of the company remaining competitive in the
global economy – but that executives were getting paid more. It was
unfair. The income gap continued to widen and it became common
knowledge that the worker was not getting a good deal. William Morris
had observed a century earlier that worthy work gives us hope, but it is
difficult today to find truly worthy work. Without worthy work, we'll
have to find hope elsewhere. With today's technology, social attitudes
and appetite for self-actualisation, we'd ideally look upon our work
with a sense of pride, involvement and accomplishment. But we're
rarely given the chance. Instead, we pretend to love our jobs with an
almost idiotic zeal, while being secretly exhausted and insulted by
them. In fact, we should treat work with honest scorn as long as work

remains inane and over-supervised and is arrived at through economic necessity alone.

This may very well be the beginning of the end for work. In the future, we'll see a widening gap between rich and poor, as jobs usually reserved for the middle classes are either automated or outsourced or simply abandoned when companies are liquidated or bankrupted by the super-rich (as was the case in the Phones4U scandal in the UK in 2014). Work becoming meaningless or hard to come by, would not be so bad if we could only learn that the eradication of work is a good thing – in fact the moment we've all been waiting for! But we will need to change our social obsession with finding identity through work, give up the idea that life without work is in some way disgraceful or indolent, and we'll need to find a way to pay everyone's bills without work: whether by abolishing the idea of property altogether or by instating Citizen's Income. This, of course, is an awful lot of history to put behind us.

## WORK AS IDENTITY

To what extent does work impact upon our identities? When we're encouraged to go through university with an ultimate career in mind (starting at the age of 18 no less!) and to keep these plans in mind when steering through a career for the next 40 or so years, the central thing to consider, if not money, does seem to be identity. We're supposed to ask 'what sort of person do I want to be?' and then to take a punt on the kind of career that could facilitate this whim. If I want to adopt the identity of a kind and dutiful carer, maybe I'll become a nurse. If I want the identity of an adventurer, maybe I'll join the Navy or the Royal Society. If I want the identity of a Machiavellian vandal, maybe I'll start shaking the clawed hands necessary to become a Conservative MP.

But can a job really determine our identity? To what extent am I an author or an office worker or librarian or a paperboy? Where do these roles meet, complement or conflict with my non-professional identities as a long-distance walker, son, friend or appreciator of filthy limericks? I'm sceptical about the effectiveness of adopting such personas and also the inherent worth of doing so.

On one hand, it might seem obvious that the activities shaping the bulk of our days – our time on Earth – play a part in how others perceive us and how we perceive ourselves. On the other, there's the intuitive feeling that there's a truer, more latent identity beneath our veneers of professionalism: that once we're stripped of the uniform at the end of a working day, we're finally free to be who we *really* are. At home, we can fart and swear and sing and bellow and get drunk and say the things we really feel. Such a display of true self is frowned upon even in the Googleplex. Moreover, now that boundaries between work and personal life are becoming increasingly blurred – since work has leaked into the home through email and social life into the office through Facebook – are we being taken over, Mr Hyde-like, by our professional avatars?

Defining ourselves through the work we do might be good deal for rock stars, footballers, poet laureates, prime ministers, supermodels and astronauts but probably not such a good deal for the majority. What if you've had the incredible misfortune to become a PE teacher? It would be degrading to accept wholeheartedly that we're minor functionaries in malign companies or that we occupy highly dispensable positions in wings of bureaucracies that don't really need to exist. We're left with a decision: to accept that work *is* a big part of identity and that therefore we truly are mediocre pen-pushers in a world shared with superstars; or to know that identity is *not* impacted by the job you do and that you're a complex universe trapped inside a toiling meat machine.

In the past, for better or worse, this question would not have needed to be asked. It's only quite recently we've decided to embrace career as identity, perhaps because there's now the suggestion of choice ('You can be anything!') and the pernicious illusion of meritocracy ('Hard work is rewarded!'). In the past, we might have been slaves with truly no choice; or gentry or aristocrats with no need for choice. More recently, we might have followed in our parents' footsteps, or inherited the family business. It's only in the post-*It's a Wonderful Life* world, in which we're encouraged to smash our apparent destinies, that we've taken to thinking of career as a kind of identity-cementing lifestyle choice. Writing at the turn of the twentieth century, when the idea of work as identity really kicked in, etiquette expert Emily Post points out how rude it is to ask people you've met socially about their day jobs. 'And what do you do?' may seem like harmless small talk but, she argues, it could equally be an ill-mannered intrusion upon a person's secret shame and is certainly a buzzkill-ish failure to leave the world of drudgery out of the party. Emily Post acknowledged that what a person does for a living is not, for better or worse, whom they are.

Identity, I'd say, is multifaceted and complex: we behave differently in different situations and with different people. The people in one pub might celebrate me as the guy who aces the quiz machine, while the people in another pub know me as the loser who can't hit the dartboard. Internally too, we have different ideas about ourselves from one day to the next: we can feel differently about ourselves depending upon what we've been eating or not eating, how much money happens to be in our bank accounts at a given moment, or what kind of books we've been reading recently. The kind of clothes we wear makes a huge difference: I'm definitely treated differently when I wear a hoodie and jeans compared with days I wear a suit. Sense of identity is all over the place: one might as well have a cabinet full of different, exchangeable, screw-on heads like Princess Mombi in *Return to Oz*. Identity is not supposed to be consistent. Unfortunately, a job serves as an unnatural consistency-enforcing device: by pulling you back to a near-identical circumstance every single day, it seals our identity one day at a time. When we're dragged through the same commuter route each morning, warm the same chair in the office for the same hours, talk to the same people and eat at the same cafeteria, there's a kind of cumulative taming effect. And so our identities – how we see ourselves and how others see us – become shaped by the workplace. At work, we become the guy who eats at *this* spot in the canteen or the woman who uses *that* hot desk. In the outside world, we slowly become Suzanne the Bus Driver or Steve the Postie or – perhaps the worst fate of all – Kanye the God.

## MY SECOND JOB

*Bang!* DECLINED. *Bang!* DECLINED. *Bang!* DECLINED. That was the sound of me rubber-stamping some documents in the job I'm about to describe. It seemed like a more theatrical opening to this bit of the book than simply trotting out the following words: in the UK, high school students complete a period of 'work experience' before graduation.

See what I mean? Boring. True and necessary, but boring. I bet you're glad I made that silly rubber-stamping gambit now. Anyway, work experience usually involves a week of unpaid grunt work or personal shadowing at a local organisation, to give the young blot-on-the-landscape a first-hand idea of what a job feels like.

I think this is a rather strange mistake on behalf of the establishment: if the education system wants to prepare high school students for the workforce, the last thing it should do is provide sneak peeks into how horrible it is. They should just line you up with a job to go into at graduation only letting you discover the horrors of work when it's too late. Having said that, everyone seems happy to go along with the existing system of walking into The Trap of their own accord even after being tipped off about it.

Some of my schoolmates took jobs in newspaper offices (one at the *Dudley News* no less), factories, video rental shops, post offices, nurseries and, most excitingly, an abattoir. Kurt, who landed this job, told us how one abattoir worker would daily put a pair of freshly-scalped pig's ears on his head like a Mickey Mouse hat from a grisly Disney World, and carry on about his duties as if everything was perfectly normal.

For my work placement, I was somehow lumbered with the office of the local council department responsible for allocating a limited number of government-owned houses to poor families. It was dull but at least it wasn't an abattoir. One afternoon, after a worker's lunch of crap sandwiches and a banana (on that note, isn't there's something uniquely bleak about the sight of a single, unitary banana in a vending machine?), I was given the task of rubber-stamping some declined applications from home seekers. Even though the applications had already been formally refused, it felt astonishingly evil to bang the word 'DECLINED' onto the handwritten pleas of desperately poor, sooty-fingered Midlanders. It wasn't their fault their skills were no longer marketable in the Ikea-furnished, post-Thatcher Dudley.

And then it happened: I came to an application from someone I knew. He'd requested a bungalow on account of his rheumatoid arthritis making stairs difficult. His proposal had already been declined, but I couldn't bring myself to rubber-stamp it for the files. I told my supervisor, vainly hoping I could get someone to reconsider, but she just stamped it herself.

Another worker, a blonde *Übermensch* called Luke, had a corner office aside from the main open-plan one. The women in the office fancied him to distraction, making him a kind of cock-of-the-walk office monkey. I wondered if this was why he had a separate office, so everyone could get some work done without the distraction of his exquisite beauty. Luke once pulled me away from some dispiriting task – rubber-stamping the word 'NO!' onto the pleas of orphans perhaps – so I might help in his office. The new task turned out to be playing solitaire on Microsoft Windows. He said that if anyone should happen to come in, I should pretend to file paperwork, and stuck a pile of old invoices in front of me to complete the illusion. Being square, I was concerned that this waste of time would stop me learning something useful. Little did I know that playing solitaire and pretending to work was the *perfect* preparation for office life. I started to suspect I'd had it pretty sweet on that paper round.

## LOST IN TRANSITION

'Slavery has been abolished, but the laws of emancipation do not touch us as we toil away in the train-gang.' Thus spake 'Tiresias', a man who commuted from Oxford to London every workday for the customary 40 years. He maintained an astonishingly literary and heartfelt note-book of commuter woe, which he eventually had published as *Notes from Overground*. 'No one writes about commuting (except incidental-ly),' he tells us, 'because no one sees it as a state or a predicament, as a valid experience.'

Commuting is lost time. Time spent in a crammed train may as well have trickled away behind the fridge, and you'll absolutely never get it back. I always saw commuting as a special form of soul torture. Not only do we have to agree to a job, but we have to physically transplant ourselves each day to the place where we're supposed to do it. Some of my darkest hours have been spent trundling along in buses or trains, working hard to reach a place I don't want to be, angry and depressed before the clock is even punched. To facilitate work, we catch rush hour buses: standing room only, clutching for dear life to a stainless steel pole or swinging from a plastic loop, surrounded by sad lottery players with the sniffles. Some try to dull the pain and hold onto some semblance of self by listening to music on iPods, but doing so is tantamount to a man overboard trying to stay afloat on a woodworm-riddled piano leg. I eventually learned it was a mistake to listen to rousing music on the way to work. After listening to 'Seven Nation Army' by the White Stripes, the sensation of reality rushing back when you unpluck the earpieces at the office is too much to bear.

People take cars onto the road at no small expense and then sit in traffic, inhaling fumes and becoming more and more anxious about everything and nothing while listening to rush hour DJs prattle on about some inane new meme or a horrible war which, from our four-wheeled prison on the M8, we're uniquely qualified to do nothing about. Some try to help the environment by carpooling, but this means the insane small talk of someone from work. Top tip: never get into polite conversation with a colleague unless there's a clear line of escape.

People catch trains: trains with their engineering interruptions and replacement bus services and indecipherable PA announcements, and all those pushy people who try to win back dignity by bullying their way ahead of the others in order to get a seat. 'Man is born free,' wrote Tiresias, 'but is everywhere in trains.' I don't have the courage to spare too much thought for the poor sods who commute by aeroplane. Imagine that. Airports and turbulence as part of the daily grind.

We usually commute because of a commonly held idea that living in a big house far away from our daily work is somehow worth striving for, when in fact it's an obvious waste of time and source of considerable misery. 'People commute reluctantly,' writes journalist and happiness expert Oliver Burkeman, 'because they can't afford to live closer to work – yet if they get rich, they're liable to do it to an even greater degree, presumably because they think living in the countryside will make them happier [but] it often doesn't...People chronically under-estimate the downsides of a long commute, while overestimating the upsides of (say) a bigger house.' Is it not bizarre that people continue to make this misdiagnosis of riches so long after the invention of suburbia and a trillion, trillion bus journeys, even into the age of the internet?

# A SHORTHAND FOR DYSTOPIA

If you're writing a novel or a film script and you want to quickly get the idea across that your character has a crap life, all you have to do sit him on an ergonomic swivel chair. The open-plan office with its incarcerated drones overseen by a swaggering moron of a manager has become the go-to literary device when it comes to illustrating the failure of modern life to cater for our happiness.

Douglas Coupland in *Generation X* described office pods as 'veal-fattening pens'. That brief and brutal description contained so much satire and accuracy that it should have been the final word on office design. We should have all said, 'Shit, he's right!' and immediately scrapped the whole idea of the open-plan office. But twenty years later we're still using it. People go to quite peculiar lengths to work in them, sweating through job interviews and torturing themselves by trying to squash a CV onto two A4 sheets. In 1999, Keanu Reeves was liberated from an open-plan office in *The Matrix*. And when he escapes and gets a peek behind the scenes of reality, he sees a field of incarcerated humans in pods, basically a sci-fi representation of the same thing.

If the open-plan office is cultural shorthand for 'environment designed to oppress humanity and destroy the spirit', why do we still have them? Nobody seems willing to accept responsibility for why the horror of offices reigns supreme. Their most likely originator, designer Bob Propst, says his invention is actually 'systems furniture' with multiple uses and that the office cubicle is an abuse of his technology. 'One of the dumbest things you can do,' he once said, 'is sit in one space and let the world pass you by.' Seriously, let's think about this for a moment. Is there any worse way of getting things done than sitting for seven hours on a swivel chair surrounded by photographs of other people's ugly children? Even if you value the basic idea of your job, your first choice of working environment is hardly going to include telephones ringing from every corner, a flickering fluorescent tube above your head and a fire drill every five minutes.

Distractions abound. In a particularly hilarious edition of the *Guardian*'s career advice column, a reader writes: 'I share an office with a woman who is in her late 30s. My problem is that she talks to herself – all day, every day. If she is writing an email she reads it out loud; if she is working on her PC she talks through the process. I have tried [everything] but she just talks louder … Help – I might just throttle her soon.' I'll bet five quid right now that the equipment you're expected to use in your office isn't even as good as the cheap Acer laptop you watch YouTube videos on at home. We tolerate nasty bulk-bought hardware, weird networking systems, and overweight software designed to spy on the worker by monitoring the websites she visits.

The office turns us into clock-watchers. What should be sacred to us – the time of our lives – is savagely broken down into hourly chunks (even half-hourly or fifteen-minute chunks if you really hate your job) as we wilfully hurry it down the plughole. We have to gawp at computers for most of the time we're at work, disconnecting us from nature and from friendly human faces. We have to humour the management speak, the snarky politics, and become apologists for other people's bad decisions. We have to get up at the crack of dawn to act as small cogs in machines with highly dubious outputs. Instead of standing on a chair to do it ourselves, we have to track down a designated light-bulb-changer who'll be rude to us and spend an hour grumpily adhering to policy simply to honour the legacy of a time-wasting bulb-changing policy the company set up three years ago. We have to sit in uncomfortable chairs, ironically twisting our spines because of an insurance policy requiring ergonomic seating for all workers.

Science fiction novelists don't have to scratch their heads for long to come up with dystopias. All they have to do is get a job in an office.

Excerpt from an SF writer's notepad: *Everyone's crammed together and secretly hates each other. Nobody can relax. Motivational drug-drinks come freely from dispensing machines. Dunder Mifflin but with tentacles.*

## MY EIGHT OR NINTH JOB

*Veeet! Veeet! 'Would you like the receipt?' 'No.' Crumple. Dump.* When I worked as a library assistant, we had a cash register at the circulation desk for the overdue charges. With each transaction, the cash register would sputter out (*veeet-veet!*) a receipt. 'Would you like the receipt?' we'd ask the punter, to which they would say 'No'. Nobody wants a receipt for a 15p library fine. So we'd tear off the receipt and put it in a little bin. The receipt bin. What a futile life that cash register had.

During a busy spell one summer afternoon, we stopped asking people whether they wanted a receipt and we stopped tearing off the receipts and we stopped putting them in the receipt bin. The receipts just kept on sputtering out uselessly and soon they formed a long chain. On one occasion, we took notice when 27 receipts had printed without breaking off. It was glorious. 'Nobody tear off a receipt!' someone said. 'Let's see how long we can get it.' It was one of those little survival techniques – little games you make up for yourselves – when you have a boring job. Sometimes, a new staff member not yet indoctrinated into the game would break the chain and put it in the bin. 'What have you done?!' we'd all shout. 'Don't break the chain!'

Sometimes, a pernickety customer would ask outright to be given a receipt and you'd be forced to break the chain. 'Are you sure you want a receipt?' you'd ask. 'Yes,' they'd say. 'Why?' you'd ask. 'Because I've spent some money and I am entitled to a receipt,' they'd say. We'd hate that person forever. If the library had been a restaurant, we'd have all gobbed in his soup. On one occasion, I saw a library assistant writing out a receipt for 50p by hand. I didn't have to ask why. She didn't want to break the chain.

Sometimes, a supervisor would tell us to stop being so silly. 'Break the chain,' he would say, 'it is a pointless mess.' Needless to say, I was suddenly driven to pass my supervisor exam as soon as possible. With me in charge, we could let the chain grow as long as we liked. The longest chain we ever cranked out was 136 receipts long. It was the most beautiful thing any of us had ever seen.

## SO WHAT'S THE POINT?

We go to work to earn money but it costs us time, meaningful relationships, and health (a 2015 study found that modern jobs can directly contribute to heart disease). Perversely, nobody ever seems to have any money. If work paid us enough, we'd never hear the words 'I can't, I'm skint'. The idea is that we work a day to fund a day (or more) of leisure later on. For most, it doesn't work that way: the only free time we get is what's granted to us in weekends and holidays and our eventual retirement (by which time your youth is gone, the prime of your life squandered and irretrievable). But at least we're all making lovely, sexy money, right? Of course not. You've never got any.

It all goes back into the economy via consumption. Chances are, it's only with you for a moment and then it's gone. Oh well. It was only a string of numbers on a screen anyway (though we don't usually see it so trivially when we're striving to earn it). The trap we seek to escape is an institutional one. It operates on a self-complementing twin mechanism. These twin components are called production and consumption – or 'work' and 'shopping' – and they support each other perfectly.

# CONSUMPTION

I hope he saved his money, for he was a clean man
with a clean reputation.
— Houdini

## MY THIRD JOB

'*Do you have a clubcard? No? Cheers. That's one pound eighty-five please.*' For better or worse, I all but grew up in a shopping mall. They started building the mall the year I was born. My parents took me shopping there when I was little. I saw movies in the cinema there as a teenager. When I turned 16, the mall gave me a Saturday job.

I worked in a two-storey super-branch of W. H. Smith. I staffed a cash register for a year but ended up running the music and video department. I'd make sure all the new-release material was prepped for Monday morning. I'd answer questions about singers and old movies that the rest of the teenage staff hadn't heard of. I'd answer the phone by saying 'Sounds', because that was the cool name of the department.

Anyway, the interesting thing about this job was getting to see behind the scenes. To the public, the mall is characterised by glistening indoor boulevards: mirrored surfaces, escalators, glistening fountains. In the Midlands of the 1980s we'd never seen anything like it. Compared to Dudley Market and the Birmingham Bull Ring, the big mall was a paradise. There were no beetroot stalks or cabbage leaves

31

underfoot. You didn't risk twisting an ankle on a poorly secured flag-stone or treading in a dog turd. The mall was like the afterlife: all of your friends were there and you could have anything you wanted.

Punching a code into a digital lock and passing through the 'staff only' door at the back of W.H. Smith, however, the shopping mall perfection gave way to an almighty stockroom that looked like Area 51. The trappings of commercial space – familiar colour schemes, piped-in pop music – abruptly gave way to concrete walls, exposed ducts and a practical military grey paint job. The soundtrack was the grunting and swearing of stockroom assistants, the crunching and screaming of heavy crates being hefted. The stockroom backed onto an exterior loading bay the size of a tennis court where trucks would arrive throughout the day, delivering stock. Upstairs was a staff room, the managerial coops, and a bank vault.

The behind-the-scenes world seemed never to end. I once lifted a ceiling tile in the staff room and found space enough for at least another floor of retail space up there. I asked an older manager about it. She explained that building a shopping mall in the Black Country – an area traditionally dedicated to heavy industry – was seen as a risky and cutting-edge business proposition. In 1982, it seemed genuinely unlike-ly that the local breed of coal miners and welders would ever be seduced into spending money they didn't have on fancy, imported goods like car phones and Big Macs. A contingency plan was, quite literally, built into the mall. Should it ever fail to make money as a retail outlet, the whole place could be gutted and re-purposed as factory space, the huge cavity above our heads able to accommodate big machines. There was also a labyrinth of maintenance corridors: I could leave Smiths through a fire escape, pass through a gloomy passage and pop up again in McDonald's or Mothercare. The corridors were wide enough to drive vans through but you'd never, never know of their existence if you didn't work there. Cutting through a corridor one December, I bumped into a depressed Santa Claus smoking through a plastic beard.

I enjoyed my knowledge of this strange Neverwhere of maintenance corridors and industrial contingency space. As a shopper I'd no idea that so much backroom dimness was necessary for a comparatively small amount of retail brilliance. The backrooms don't *facilitate* the mall though: they *are* the mall. Backrooms aren't backrooms: the 'front of house' is just a specialised part of the mall's anatomy evolved to lure the little fishes in. What seemed from the outside a temple of leisure – shops and cinemas and marble – was predominantly a workplace, one in which shoppers obliviously participate thanks to window dressing and cheerful muzak.

This is perhaps the most important thing to understand about The Trap: it has at its core a twin locking mechanism, two interlocking parts. We go to work to make money and then we spend it by shopping. If we didn't need so much money, we wouldn't have to work so much. If we didn't work so much, we wouldn't spend so much money. In deciding upon the structure of this book, I wasn't sure if I should put the chapter about work before the one about consumption or *vice versa* since they're so interconnected. I chose to put work first because, as I saw it, we earn money before spending it. But as my wife points out, that's a rather old-fashioned point of view. Most people today, she says, spend their money before they've earned it, going to work to pay for what they've already spent on credit cards. However true this is – whether we're a world of credit slaves or a wage slaves – work and consumption are perfectly interconnected. Once you know this, a mechanism of The Trap reveals itself. None of this is news to economists. Economically speaking, work and consumption aren't just connected but the same process seen from opposite ends. Your consumption is someone's work, your work someone's consumption. A country's GDP can be calculated by totalling the nation's earnings or the nation's consumption: both sums are the same. This will be mind-blowing information if you're one of the millions who hate their jobs and try to reclaim some dignity by buying cool stuff. Shopping is a welcome break from work – one you've literally earned – and an activity where you're in charge and attended to, instead of being pushed around by a boss, but so far as the economy's concerned, it's the same thing. Whether shopping or working, we're serving the economy where, one might add, the economy should be serving us. Whether spending or earning, we participate in the same waste of time and energy that prevents us from being free.

## THE THINGS WE WANT

For the last few Christmases, I've been part of a gift exchange with my wife's family. This poses a small problem, as I don't particularly enjoy receiving surprise gifts or shopping for them, but it'd be socially awful not to participate. For two years, I tried to promote consumable gifts via a selection of fancy soaps and a gift certificate for a hot shave at a nearby barbershop. Alas, people didn't really appreciate the non-materialist gifts. I'd missed the spirit of the gift exchange. They wanted fun stuff for immediate gratification. The most popular gift one year was from cousin Mitchell who'd had his own face printed onto a cushion. Admittedly, it was pretty funny.

So this year, we bought our gifts from a big chain bookshop. As a bookshop, I'd find it more palatable than a trip to the mall, but they also sold toys and had a kitchenware department. Why a bookshop should sell toys and kitchenware is a question I'm not qualified to answer, but stock them they did and it enabled us to buy for the gift exchange a Battleship game and a miniature kitchen blowtorch (both of which were met lacklustrely by the family – no pleasing some people). Anyway, here's a list of items I saw for sale in a 'decorative objects' department of this bookshop:

- A ceramic model of a tortoise
- A magnifying glass, the handle of which was an owl
- Various money boxes (the perfect gift for life in a cashless society)
- Novelty kitchen timers
- Another magnifying glass, the handle of which was a quill
- Sequinned pencil pots (ideal for the digital age)
- Expensive tea sampler sets
- A pack of Aubrey Hepburn-themed playing cards
- Yet another magnifying glass, the handle of which was the Eiffel Tower
- A teapot in the shape of a square of chocolate
- A tasteful milk jug in the shape of the human tit

I don't mean to be a complete killjoy, but I can't help think about how these objects ultimately come from the Earth. Raw materials and human labour were required to conjure them into existence. Orangutans die so we can have magnifying glasses with variously shaped handles. Is that acceptable? 'We have a responsibility,' said Carl Sagan, 'to deal more kindly with one another and to preserve and cherish the only home we've ever known.' We agree with this in principle, nodding until our heads are ready to fall off, but go out and buy one of those chocolate-shaped teapots. Perhaps we're within our rights to be mass consumers. If we've earned the money, surely we should be able to spend it however we please. Well, yes. But also no. On account of the fact that mass consumption is wrecking the planet.

The most obvious cost of consumption is climate change. Climate change is a daily fixture in the news now and is a reality we're all struggling with. It can be hard to comprehend the connection between personal consumption and climate change. When we buy something, we create a market for further raw material extraction and further burning of fossil fuels. Buying that hilarious milk jug in the shape of a tit contributes to climate change, but we too often don't see that because it seems quintessentially absurd. According to the Worldwide Fund for Nature, we're losing between 10,000 and 100,000 animal species each year, partly through climate change but more generally through business and development. That's between a thousand and ten thousand times higher than the natural extinction rate. In other words, human activity has been responsible for an unthinkable death toll. Human activity is work and consumption. This statistic should be reason alone to stop working and consuming so much.

The survival of biodiversity is also *our* survival. We're going the right way about making the planet uninhabitable for any form of life: human, animal, or economic. This is slowly becoming a cultural narrative but the connection between the planet's destruction and product worship still hasn't picked up the traction it needs: that or we would simply *prefer* to have stuff instead of orang-utans or a planet with a future. It's a choice and I don't mean to say it's an obvious one: the destruction of all life on Earth might conceivably be a worthy sacrifice for *something*. But, in my opinion, not iPhones or tit-shaped milk jugs.

Every human-made commodity has, at some point, come out of the ground. Every piece of plastic or paper or digital property originates in the finite raw materials of planet Earth. E. F. Schumacher in *Small is Beautiful* describes Earth's natural resources as the capital of our business. Capital – the initial injection of cash to get things going – cannot be depended upon indefinitely, but rather invested in pursuit of long-term solutions. In the case of our planet, we should be investing in sustainable ways of ensuring our future quality of life, investing in things like green energy. If energy were infinite and non-damaging, we'd be justified in having all the consumer crap we want, but we've not yet arrived at that point. As it stands, we're squandering our limited capital on short-term commercial gratification. That's like a company director throwing an epic office party when she should be hiring staff or buying equipment.

The ultimate negative consequence of consumption – if this is not too esoteric a point – is that it's distracting humanity from accomplishing things of worth. I don't know exactly what those things of worth might be, but I have an optimistic inkling that the pinnacle of human civilisation does not have to be the consumer economy. It just doesn't seem *enough*, given that we've proved ourselves so capable with Jane Austen and Shakespeare, Marie Curie and Stephen Jay Gould. Should consumerism be the last thing we accomplish as a species, after all this evolution and the miraculous series of accidents that granted our sentience? Would that not be an utterly dull and inane end to our history? Could we not now *soar*? Could we not *excel* in some way beyond the plastic and the commercial? There's an entire universe to look out at, and seven million other universes to look in on. There's international peace to find, art to make, almost infinitely renewable energies to harness, sensory pleasures both simple and complex to enjoy. Could we use science to communicate with chimps or octopods? Could we use religion to surf the seas of the soul? There are accomplishments artistic, scientific, spiritual, that nobody currently alive has even thought of and it would be a shame for the species to burn out before that person has a shot at being born. At the very least, could we not clean up after ourselves and let other kinds of life, non-human life, thrive and soar and excel after we've gone?

We buy the essentials of life like food and shelter, and conveniences like computers and phones, but we also apparently buy things like the tit jug or one of those magnifying glasses. Now that we live in the future, we can also buy less tangible commodities like gym memberships, flights, cosmetic surgery, taxi rides, downloadable applications to solve problems that didn't exist yesterday. The list is endless because as long as Capitalism keeps coming up with new stuff for us to consume, we'll keep consuming it.

Consumption has become a way of life. We shop without thinking about it. *Adbusters* editor Kalle Lasn explains how difficult some people find International Buy Nothing Day: 'It's as hard as giving up smoking for some people. [It's hard to resist] the urge to have a coffee or a Mars bar [and] people go through a cold turkey experience. They sweat, and they realise to what extent this impulse to buy is an addiction.' If our consumer desires were simply to clothe ourselves becomingly, to eat well, and to have a dignified living space, consumption wouldn't be a problem. If we wanted only those things, perhaps we'd only need to work one or two days per week. That we might know when to stop was the oversight of economists of the 1930s – Keynes, Robinson, Schumpeter – who imagined an all but work-free utopia by 2030. By embracing an industrial system, they thought they were making sacrifices for future generations, that their hard work would eventually pay off, but they did not take into account the insatiability of their descendants. The people of the 1930s knew little of planned obsolescence, tight fashion cycles, the extent of commercial appetites. Today it's not enough to have a personal portable telephone but barely enough to have *this year's* personal portable telephone. Overthrowing this insatiability is key if we're to escape consumerism. I'm not advocating a return to pre-industrial consumerist tastes, but does anyone really need a gym ball or one of those coffee pod machine thingies or a singing refrigerator?

## A MISDIAGNOSIS OF RICHES

But what if shopping and owning lots of stuff makes us happy? Happiness is important. Maybe it's enough to justify the environmental costs so long as we understand and accept them. Perhaps it's okay to turn the oceans into plastic soup if human happiness is at stake. Consider the haters who leave aggressive messages on Bea Johnson's

blog. The Johnson family have a zero waste home. They've c̣.
problem of domestic waste and now Bea runs a website to show ḥ.
done. It's a good idea: why generate waste if it can be avoided? Thḷ
no advantage to throwing food or packaging in the bin. In eliminating
waste, everybody wins. And yet she has those haters. People can react
violently when you suggest they curb what they see as consumer
freedoms. What's interesting in this instance is how many of Bea's
detractors use the word 'pleasure' in their complaints. 'Don't try to
reduce my pleasure,' they say, and 'Pleasure is too important to live as
you do'. They associate minimising waste with minimising pleasure.

The problem is that consumption has been confused with pleasure.
Capitalism has noted what humans find pleasurable – sex, eating,
community, play, personal distinction – and sold them to us in com-
modified forms. The instinct to *do* has become confused with the
instinct to *buy*. The instinct to exercise gets mixed up with the instinct
to buy the associated clothing, guidebooks, and paraphernalia. The
instinct to have sex leads to the purchase of beauty products, clothes,
cars, gizmos. You don't need any of it. It's crap. You can go for a run
without the spandex pants or an iPod. You're sexy without the peacock-
feather signifiers of wealth. You know who is sexiest? Naked people.
And they don't have *anything*.

Advertising takes advantage of the pleasure principle, aligning
products with pleasure-inducing images. Consider those nauseating
soft drink adverts that come on television around Christmas, the
one with the lorries driving through a snow-capped town and with all
the bright-eyed neighbours running out into the street to rejoice in the
coming of the cola. It shouldn't need pointing out that a fizzy brown
drink has precisely nothing to do with community or giving or
Christmas.

Pleasure is part of the basic package of life. It could be achieved in
the wild, without civilisation or an economy and certainly without
carbonated beverages. There's no need to buy pleasure or work particu-

larly hard for it. It's there, in the natural state, for free, as we'll discuss in Chapter 10. Big consumption does not result in big pleasure. Do we experience pleasure by preparing too much food and then throwing the excess in the bin? Does anyone get their rocks off by buying plastic wrapped vegetables instead of loose ones? Does drinking freshly squeezed orange juice in place of juice from a carton deny your orgasms somehow? I can't see how. I don't think Bea Johnson's detractors would think so either, but they don't get so far as asking those questions. All they see is the erroneous equation that big consumption equals big pleasure. It doesn't. Let us dismiss that myth now and forever.

Even among those sophisticated enough not to leave nasty comments on the blogs of wise young women, the pleasure/consumption mix-up takes place. There are suggestions as to why people have so much stuff. There's the commonly-held idea that we're brainwashed by advertising, but it's been proven that advertising doesn't actually work so well and that big companies mainly buy advertising as a kind of tax dodge. There's also a famine instinct theory that people are prone to hoarding, believing it to be advantageous to stock up when a good offer presents itself but forgetting that there are *always* good offers thanks to mass production and competitive marketing.

My take has more respect for human agency but admittedly questions our diagnostic abilities. I believe we identify the wrong things as riches, that we mistake certain trappings of wealth for wealth itself. There are real advantages to money: space, time, peace, privacy, and better health. Rich people's money can have the pleasing effect of lifting them from the struggle, the servitude and the ill health that tends to come with poverty. But for some reason, those without money fixate on other things about the wealthy lifestyle: the stuff. We've come to associate wealth with stuff. It seems that people eventually take the 'space, time, peace, privacy and health' but only after a massive detour via stuff. After filling ostentatious houses with crap, people retire at

70 and say 'you know, what matters most are family and health'. Well, duh.

'Space, time, peace, privacy and health' don't necessarily cost much if we go directly to them instead of via the life-long acquisitional detour. Stuff is unimportant. Much of it doesn't give you pleasure. You have to work for it or fall into debt for it, so it actually provides misery.

Studies show that money can buy happiness but only up to a certain level of income. When a family unit reaches an annual income of around £44,000 or £22,000 per person nothing can be done, materially, to increase their happiness any further. There's also the phenomenon of *relative* income to consider: so long as you're earning as much as (or slightly more than) your significant peers then you'll probably be happy no matter what level of the pay scale you all happen to be at. As long as you don't feel poor in comparison to the quality of life you observe among your peers, you'll feel relatively wealthy. In his book, *Enough*, journalist John Naish suggests that the secret of material contentment is stay on or slightly above the median earning level for your country. In the UK, the average weekly income is £355. That's the price, it seems, of maximum material happiness. If you're paying more (working more hours per week than it takes to make £355) then you're getting ripped off. If we were wise, we'd work until the hour of £355 some time on Wednesday morning, immediately put our jackets on and walk out of the building.

If we find ourselves lusting after expensive products, we'll be motivated to spend more time on the bus and in the office to pay for them. That way, my friends, madness lies: we end up putting in the hours to fund a commodity-centric lifestyle that will not make us happy. Worse, if the hours we work are still not enough to fund our appetites, we can fall into debt.

# DEBT

Debt is the opposite of freedom. It would make sense to avoid it at all costs, but we're encouraged by banks and mortgage providers to go into debt. A common enough willingness to go into debt to maximise consumption is a staggering triumph of commodity lust over reason. If consumption and work are the central twin mechanism of The Trap, debt is a kind of annex mechanism, an enhancement of the consumption wheel. Consumption creates a need for work, and the facility to run into debt exacerbates this relationship. Not only can an appetite for consumption lead to wage slavery but we can find ourselves in the position of working to pay for things enjoyed in the past. If you have a blowout on Day 1, you can still be paying for it by Day 100. This truly is the modern equivalent of indentured servitude: a system wherein a poor European would agree to work five years or more in exchange for passage to the New World. At least those slaves had the promise of a better future. Today's wage slaves are paying for their past.

It seems to begin these days with student loans. This is how they get you. It should be illegal. A student loan normalises the idea of debt, flings us into it at a young age and we become more willing to take other loans because of it. Before we've paid off a student loan, we land a mortgage and credit card debt and before we know it we're applying for a high-interest loan from a highly dubious outfit like Wonga. Apparently it's common for people of my generation, currently in their early thirties, to have barely made a dent in repaying their student loan thanks in part to low incomes but also to the interest continually being applied by the loans company. Is it not disgraceful that such skulduggery is allowed to happen at all, let alone be accepted as normal?

The debt market is populated by heinous predators preying on society's most vulnerable. A Google search for the word 'debt' immediately results in a large number of suspect links for consolidation firms and dodgy-looking lending plans.

A football-loving friend mentions Manchester United's debt problems. 'I'll stop you there,' I say, '*Football*'. We have a long history of his raising footballing topics and my immediately glazing over. I thought I'd successfully negotiated a truce, but there we were. 'Not football,' he says, '*Finance*. Manchester United is one of the biggest companies in the world.' How can one of the biggest companies in the world have debt problems? How can it be that Manchester United's combined footballing and business prowess has succeeded in landing their organisation in debt? Moreover, in what way can Manchester United be 'one of the biggest companies in the world' if they are in debt? Debt is *negative money*. If Manchester United is so much as £1 in debt, they're a smaller company than I am. How can one be anywhere between Salford and Dar es Salaam and find someone wearing the familiar red shirt of Manchester United when the organisation apparently has less actual money than I do? It's because we live in a debt economy. The richest person or organisation is not the one with the most money in the bank (or invested in stocks or under the bed in a crusty sock) but the one with the most purchasing power. In other words, the richest person or organisation is the one who is able to accrue the most debt. A bank will give Man U a multi-million-pound loan for the same reason they're unlikely to give one to me: because lending to Manchester United will make them money.

Companies and nations fall over each other in an attempt to win the most purchasing power. Today's equivalent to the Cold War is probably America and China's ongoing contest to become the nation with the most purchasing power. The effect of this trickles down to every one of us: they push us into work in order to increase GDP, in turn helping our countries to borrow more money from other countries. And then the newspapers run stories about 'the national deficit' and how it means there's no money for healthcare or education or any other worthy pursuits and that austerity measures will have to be made. This is why so many rich people are basically off their rockers. It's because they're central players in a world of incomprehensible levels of debt, and vessels of the magnificent anxiety that must come with that. They must simultaneously accept loans in order to maximise purchasing power and fret about what will happen if they fail to pay them back.

Money lending – usury – in the ancient world was usually forbidden. In *The Divine Comedy* Dante places the usurers in the inner ring of the seventh circle of Hell: 'Man is meant to earn his way and further humankind. But still the usurer takes another way: he scorns nature and her follower, art.'

In a novel called *The Music of Chance* by Paul Auster, the protagonist must pay gambling debts to a pair of eccentric millionaires. Since he doesn't have the money, the millionaires suggest he pays in labour by building a stone wall on their property, using ten thousand heavy stones formerly of a ruined Irish castle. The wall itself is meaningless, a folly, since it fulfils no practical purpose and nobody will ever witness its majesty, but our poor fellow must build it anyway in order to pay his debts. He finds himself, for 50 days, a debt slave. Is this not the situation in which most of us find ourselves today? Auster's absurd vision served as a metaphor in 1990 but today it's a reality for those who accepted student loans and now toil away in supermarkets or offices into their thirties or forties to pay it off. Student loansters don't even have stone walls to show for it: any time put into price-tagging shelves in Tesco is quite simply *gone*. They don't even get the exercise that would come with building a wall, or the potential pride in a job completed, and they certainly can't walk away after 50 days. Debt slavery is illegal under international law. Yet here we are, toiling in meaningless jobs – more meaningless than building a stone wall – to pay debts we should never have been sold. Debt breeds anxiety, commits the bearer to years of servitude, and creates an insane international situation. Debt helps nobody. It is the reverse of freedom. It has brought new strength to The Trap.

The market is a useful system for making available the food and clothes and the other things we need for a dignified life, but it also has a tendency to seduce us with *stuff*. Stuff can bring us nothing like real pleasure or real happiness and contributes to environmental strife. To respond to stuff is to fall victim to a lure. We all know this intuitively and shouldn't need scientific studies or smart arses like me to tell us so. But in a world where we've confused the desirable 'space, time, peace, privacy and health' of affluence with the meaningless materialism it can also come with, it does seem like it needs pointing out.

Ownership of stuff is more likely to obstruct our way to freedom than contribute to it. It fortifies The Trap. You are not the sum of the things you own or the buying power you've achieved by signing up to mortgages or improving your credit rating. You can only improve your life and the lives of those around you by being a better person. Your best chance at becoming a better person, I believe, lies in becoming a *freer* person and from there being able to, as Oscar Wilde put it, 'realise the perfection of the soul within'. There is nothing you can buy that will make you better or freer. You are enough.

# 3

# BUREAUCRACY

I was placed in the great vault usually assigned to political
prisoners, and when the great door was shut, I had the
hardest time of my life, perhaps, in releasing myself.
But nevertheless, it took me eighteen minutes
to walk out, and face the dazed officials.
— Houdini

## THE TYRANNY OF FORM FILLING

Bureaucracy destroys initiative. It cannot abide innovation, revolution or direct action. It exists almost exclusively to hamper these things, to slow them down, to stop free and experimental living. And doesn't it seem that bureaucracy's encroaching further and further? Doesn't it seem that what freedom we might have outside of work and consumption is slowly being gobbled up by new kinds of digital paperwork? It's baffling how so many of us have been convinced to sit around, voluntarily entering our personal details into forms, as if that were some kind of entertaining leisure pursuit. It's also odd that we spend so much time listening to placating music down telephone receivers and using dinner parties as places to sound off about expensive or under-delivering *data plans* when we could be languishing or laughing or exchanging ideas.

On the surface, it's in our best interests to cooperate with admin – to spend some time hacking at paperwork today to buy freedom tomorrow – but tomorrow never seems to come because paperwork generates more paperwork. It's like a Hydra: lop off one head and another six really pissed-off ones grow in its place. We have bills to pay, tax to pay, exceptions to wangle, discounts to apply for: perhaps not objectionable actions in themselves, but it's annoying how they combine to form a super-build-up of bureaucracy, like plaque on a tooth or one of those 'fatbergs' that threaten to block London sewers. It may be easy enough – just 10 minutes of application – to pay an electricity bill, but the company will send one every month, and various bits of advertising and second-guessing and meter-reading and receipt-issuing in the meantime. Bell, the dominant telephone company in Canada, is like a jilted boyfriend who won't take a hint, sending us love letters about their new products every five minutes. *You installed our phone line*, I always think, *that's the extent of our relationship. Now go away.* The electricity people are similarly needy and so can be the telly people, the gas people, the tax people, etc., etc. Bureaucracy accumulates and becomes a constant, ever-present nuisance.

If we want to do something perfectly normal, like go to university or get a job, an amount of organisational admin falls to us. Given that we probably don't really want to go to university or get a job in the first place (when considering university or a job, we're already humouring the system by doing what it demands of us) it's a bit rich that it should fill up our pre-student or pre-employment time with paperwork too. There are UCAS forms to complete, references to gather, CVs to perfect, listings to peruse, people to schmooze. None of this is fun or free and we're not being paid or learning anything yet. If we want to do something relatively *un*usual – build a house, go in for alternative schooling – there's even more paperwork. In fact, the more unusual the activity, the more paperwork there will be: a clear indication that those in power don't want us to do anything unusual. They don't want us to escape, to be outliers, because we'd be harder to govern and more difficult to juice for money and labour. The way they make it difficult without directly outlawing these activities is to put bureaucratic obstacles in place. You come to the end of a form only to find the words 'please fax this form to …'. *Fax?!* This isn't because someone in an office genuinely thinks fax is the best and most convenient way to communicate. They're protecting themselves from the angry or disenfranchised or hungry people wanting their heads on platters. Make no mistake, bureaucracy serves the few and the strong. It does not serve us, the weaker majority. This is how bureaucracy is part of the mechanism of The Trap.

Bureaucracy, like the Slenderman, is scary because it has no face. This facelessness – the fact that there's nothing recognisably human about it, nothing we can appeal to or reason with – is why there are thousands of perfectly innocent people banged up in American mega-prisons and places like Guantánamo Bay without trial, interminably waiting to see whether they'll be allowed back into the real world. An altercation with a cop or airport security agent or a simple misunderstanding has genuinely put people behind bars, prevented from standing trial because of 'backlog'. Bureaucratic inefficiency has the potential to seriously get in the way of people's lives. Anyone who's tried to honour the law by applying for something as simple a fishing permit or a busking licence (isn't it weird that you're supposed to do paperwork if you want to play the harmonica outdoors with a hat in front of you?) will know that it's a headache. Try something more ambitious like immigration to another country or starting a community garden on some unused wasteland, and you can find yourself in bureaucratic imbroglio.

Bureaucracy encourages, even requires, demographic thinking. In real life, this is not helpful. At best it introduces an inconvenience to be danced around. At worst, it creates and continues to define social rifts. Social rifts are dangerous. Bureaucracy loves a social rift. One minute you're completing a census, the next you're being shot in a field. There's a detention centre in Papua New Guinea where, at the time of writing this book, over a thousand refugees are held on behalf of the Australian government. It's not called a 'prison' or even a 'detention centre'. It's called the Manus Island Regional Processing Centre, which tells you all you need to know about bureaucracy.

IBM technology and their willingness to do business with the Nazi government facilitated the running of concentration camps in the 1940s. IBM stands for International Business Machines, a top-notch bureaucratic euphemism for concentration camps. The systematic murder and disposal of over 11 million people would have been difficult to accomplish this without a super-slick bureaucracy. It's telling how slow, complicated and inefficient bureaucracy will inevitably be when it comes to catching wealthy tax dodgers or helping non-wealthy individuals to get things done; and how lubricated, simple and efficient it will be when aiding the authorities in detecting minor benefit fraud, kicking migrants out of the country or bulldozing starved corpses into a big pit. We should treat bureaucracy with absolute suspicion. It controls our actions and creates barriers to liberty. Whatever it serves, it's not life and it's not freedom.

My most full-on encounter with what we might call the 'bureaucratic absurd' has been in trying to move from Britain to Canada. 'The greatest escape I ever made,' said Houdini, 'was when I left Appleton, Wisconsin.' He might not have intended this as a slur against his hometown but as a comment on how needlessly tricky it can be to move from one place to another. My own escape from one place to another has been complicated and expensive from Day One. I'll not tell you the whole story because it seems so unbelievable now that a full account would drive us both insane. I could tell you how the complicated application forms required me to do strange things like call up old school teachers and the GCSE exam boards to request signed 'attestations'. I could tell you about the year of silence that came after getting the receipt for my application and about how we phoned the immigration authorities to ask what's going on (in defiance of their strongly-worded instruction not to call them lest it 'delay the decision on my application') to find that my application had been misplaced and that processing had not even begun. I could tell you about how, when I was eventually granted an immigration interview, I had to fly all the way to France at a few day's notice, just after Christmas, even though there was a perfectly good *Immigration Québec* office just around the corner from my apartment in Montreal (my 'local' office, since I'd applied from the UK, was the Paris branch). And I could, if you're a real kinky-pants, tell you about the time we found their helpline number alternately went nowhere or to a government voicemail message about a seal cull. But I can't bear to tell you everything: they're tales that witness madness. The official process of immigration took three years.

Unfortunately, those who venture into self-employment will face a lot of bureaucracy. We're supposed to register our companies and to keep our own accounts: it's not enough to simply start working on something interesting and reaping any rewards that might come with it. This, along with the necessary funding applications and the ongoing search for clients, inconveniences Escapologists. It can be hard, bureaucratically speaking, to go it alone.


## GOVERNMENT


Government allows us to enjoy an artificial sense of freedom (study, work, shop, retire, die) but makes it difficult to accomplish things of real worth. The purpose of government is to restrict the movement and behaviour of people. Like an orthodontist using a brace to adjust a teenager's wonky teeth, a government uses the systems of law and law enforcement to dictate the shape of the society over which it has assumed control. Government is sadism at the official level. It's something of a mystery that anyone trusts government (and according to Caroline Lucas's brilliant 2015 book, *Honourable Friends?: Parliament and the Fight for Change*, public trust in MPs has never been lower). and that anyone would vote for a major political party or indeed at all.

Government has failed us time and again. They've forged corrupt relationships with corporations. They're the ones who litter the landscape with bureaucracy, like bear traps, to stop us from coming and going freely.

Bureaucracy is at once the tool of government and the environment in which it swims. A dictionary definition of bureaucracy – 'the structure and regulations in place to control activity' – is almost inseparable from 'government'. As Escapologists, we do not want our activities to be controlled and we do not seek (or frankly consent) to be governed. The government even monitor our emails and phone calls: this is no longer a paranoid conspiracy theory but an accurate description of reality. In 2013, a bit of government called the GCHQ received considerable media attention when Edward Snowden revealed that the agency were collecting all online personal data in the UK via the sinisterly-named Tempora Programme. Despite being outed by brave Snowden, the Orwellian practice continues in the name of public safety.

It'd be hard to get rid of government if we didn't want it. Somehow, in the UK at least, the government have engineered an electoral system called 'First Past the Post' in which it's almost impossible for us to get rid of either of the main parties. It enforces a two-party system, meaning that if the opposition is essentially the same as the governing party, there's not very much we can do about it. The ramifications of this are huge. We do not have anything like a proper democracy. The government have ditched democracy because democracy would be contrary to their interests. This is what Emma Goldman meant when she said 'if voting changed anything, it would be illegal'.

The government are not our friends. Sartre said 'Freedom is what you do with what's been done to you' and the government are the most powerful purveyors of 'doing to you'. Bureaucracy is how they do it. Bureaucracy is part of The Trap, a reinforcement mechanism that makes it difficult to escape the work-and-consumption double-locking mechanism. The Trap is like a fortress complex where, if you were to escape the dungeon and bypass the portcullis, you'd still have to vault the moat. Escapologists will be confronted by the moat – bureaucracy – once they've escaped the work-and-consumption edifice but it's worth remembering that we're prey to bureaucracy anyway: it can knock on our door any time it feels like it, no matter how well we've served The Trap. We might as well grapple with bureaucracy productively as part of an escape bid instead of fumbling with it worthlessly in a day job.

# OUR STUPID, STUPID BRAINS

When I am stripped and manacled, nailed securely within a
weighted packing case and thrown into the sea, or when
I am buried alive under six feet of earth, it is necessary
to preserve absolute serenity of spirit . . .
If I grow panicky I am lost.
— Houdini

## CAVEMAN BRAIN

Where work and consumption are externally generated,
plonked in our laps by culture or other people, another part
of The Trap is internally generated: psychological foibles.
Evolutionary psychologists explain the problem: we have old brains
in a new world. Our brains evolved in a natural environment, one now
enhanced and augmented by culture and technology. We have caveman
brains in a digital world, which is why we're prone to things like over-
eating, hoarding, sexual opportunism, ambition. There's no shortage
of material wealth in the West today — we have too much — but the
caveman brain doesn't see it that way. Our brains are still cautious and
fearful, even in this world of sexy, glitzy plenty.

What generates these fears and foibles is an evolutionary vestige.
It's like a wisdom tooth or an appendix. We don't need it. It can cause
problems. The hopes and fears of the caveman brain reinforce The Trap

and hamper our escape. When we spend hard-earned money on the kinds of short-term convenience appealing to the caveman brain (ready meals, taxicabs, bank overdrafts) we're being forced to work longer to pay for those bad habits. Escape edges further away. It can be hard, when we're in The Trap to break these bad habits. It's hard to overrule them when we're tired or feeling low, which is how The Trap succeeds in making us feel. In *The Road to Wigan Pier*, George Orwell writes 'When you are [...] harassed, bored, and miserable, you don't want to eat dull wholesome food. You want something a little bit tasty. There is always some cheaply pleasant thing to tempt you.' He goes on to describe the physical defects and health issues that trouble the working classes as a result of this attraction to short-term palliatives: shit teeth, bad posture, spiritual corrosion. Proponents of The Trap – those who benefit from our being full-time, round-the-clock workers and consumers – are grateful for our bad habits and weaknesses and our tendency to procrastination. It's possible they actively encourage us to fall into those bad habits in the first place so that we stay trapped for as long as possible (though as Orwell had it, 'what I have seen of our governing class does not convince me that they have that much intelligence').

Whether the establishment is responsible for our oppressive weakness or simply grateful for it, it's possible for us to be masters of our private thoughts and to show those managers and politicians and dads, who is, in fact, the boss. We don't even have to become Buddhists or Vulcans if we don't want to. First know this. You're not tired. You're not broken. You're not weak. It's an illusion. We each have the energy, resolve and strength to break or pick the manacles. The manacles are, and always were, imaginary and it's always possible to imagine an equally imaginary, but more victorious, hacksaw or lock pick. Let's have a quick look at the psychological issues that most contribute to our ensnarement in The Trap.

## BAD FAITH

'We don't do the things we want to do,' wrote Orwell in *Coming Up for Air*. 'There's some devil in us that drives us to and fro on everlasting idiocies. There's time for everything except the things worth doing.' Why is this, eh? Why should it be the case that we dwell on these 'everlasting idiocies'? One suggestion comes from Jean-Paul Sartre who suggests we're too often crushed by 'Bad Faith': a form of self-delusion about our free will. It's actually quite scary to have free will, to have unlimited options. Before he was an author, Roald Dahl worked as a salesperson for the Shell Corporation, and wrote of his time there, 'I began to realise how simple life could be if one had a regular routine to follow with fixed hours and a fixed salary and very little original thinking to do. The life of a writer is absolute hell compared with the life of a businessman. The writer has to force himself to work. He has to make his own hours and if he doesn't go to his desk at all there is nobody to scald him . . . a person is a fool to become a writer. His only compensation is absolute freedom.'

This is perhaps one of the challenges of Escapology: there's always something deliberate and self-initiated to do when you're free and your survival may well depend on it. In a conventional job, your routines and thoughts and motivations are catered for and one can take solace in being a robot if one wants to. To sidestep the terrifying reality of 'absolute freedom' and the obligation to act for ourselves, we tend to come up with excuses to help us deny the reality of free will. It's easier and less scary to point to our shackles and say 'I can't come to Beijing because I'm trapped. Nope, nothing I can do'.

In Bad Faith, we convince ourselves that the world of The Trap is hunky-dory. We say 'everyone does this' or 'I'd be bored without it' or 'there's no choice'. Sartre observes a waiter in a restaurant who acts strangely: deliberately, ostentatiously laying the silverware and attending to the diners obsequiously. The reason, Sartre suggests, is that he's trying extra hard to be a waiter. He's exhibiting Bad Faith: quashing his own true self in order to fulfil the role of waiter. Through his actions he deceives himself: 'I'm not *Pierre* – a free man and a finely evolved primate – while I enact these motions, I am *the waiter*'. He denies his freedom as a kind of defence mechanism.

Bad Faith more generally is to deliberately betray the spirit of an agreement. Sartre used the term to highlight the gravity of the self-betrayal when a person denies his or her own complete self. Like it or not, human beings are usually born free. The things that make us feel trapped are imaginary: debt, career, social status, expectations. We can overcome these things at the drop of a decision, but we tend not to because of an imagined duty toward them and a fear of absolute freedom. It would be disingenuous to say, 'Oh, they're just imaginary and therefore not a problem', but it would be equally disingenuous to accept them as ultra-real and impervious to being escaped with anything greater than an equal response of imagination. Bad Faith is the natural enemy of Escapologists, because it is one of the main powers preventing us from silently walking out of our offices, never to return. But, as we'll see later, we *can* escape it.

## RESISTANCE

Another clue about Orwell's 'everlasting idiocies' comes from a novelist called Steven Pressfield. He battles each day, he says, with 'Resistance' (always with a capital 'R'). Resistance is the voice in our heads that tells us to do the laundry or alphabetise our tie collection or some other ludicrous form of 'clearing the deck' instead of tackling our real projects – escape plans, novels, self-improvement – head on. Resistance is the force that causes us to defer or distract ourselves from activities that might actually be beneficial.

You've probably faced Resistance if you've ever tried to write a book, to set up a business, to get fit or healthy. Anything worth doing, as well as being made difficult by the exterior forces of bureaucracy and consumption and having to go to work, is met with Resistance from within. The means of escaping Resistance are spelled out simply and clearly by Steven Pressfield in his neat little book *The War of Art*. He encourages the reader to see Resistance as an army of demons or dragons or 'alien visitations'. This exercise in fantasy is useful, partly as a way to present Resistance as defeatable – we can be the knights who kill the dragons, the slayers who lop the heads off demons – but also as a way of understanding how voices of Resistance, while internally-generated, aren't really *us*. The voices of Resistance are voices of *doubt* and they want to stop us from doing anything worthwhile. We defeat them, says Pressfield, by 'turning pro'. A pro, he says, shows up. A pro puts in the hours. A pro stays on the job for as long as there's work to be done. Bit by bit, we push the forces of Resistance into retreat simply by showing up and fulfilling our self-designed duties. When we sit in that chair and do what we're supposed to be doing, we're in a gun turret taking out the encroaching hordes or on our faithful steed broadswording those nagging orcs into pulp.

The war-against-Resistance technique can be applied to any project where self-motivation is the key or where our own hesitation is likely to hold us back: forming and acting on our escape plans, for example. We must show up each day. We must tend to our escape plans. We must pick another lock to let another chain fall away. We must add more money to the escape fund. We must brush up on the skills we'll need after escaping. We must exercise our free will. We must conduct exercises in fear setting and perspective shifting. We must cultivate our idea of freedom. Each action pushes back against the forces of Resistance. *We show up each day*. Millions do it for far less.

The only people who profit from our Resistance are the ones who want to see us warming a swivel chair in a cubicle at 9am or pushing a trolley around the aisles on Saturday mornings when we could be in bed or enjoying our freedom. They want our obedience, our time and our energy. They love our Resistance. They kiss it and want to marry it. A strike against our Resistance is a strike against *them*. Push them back, I say, inch by inch.

Needless to say, all of this 'pro' business and army metaphor isn't immediately appealing to a vegetarian sausage like me. It's masculine, fight-oriented and professional sounding. My natural inclination is to approach the world from a perspective of play and nonsense and flightiness. But there's something very powerful about Steven Pressfield's strategy and it can get us over a difficult hump when we need it to. It highlights the fact that pulling the trigger on an escape plan isn't necessarily easy. It could be a struggle and some fears will have to be confronted. Sometimes we'll have to grasp the nettle. Sometimes there really is work to be done: finding the courage to hand in our notice, drumming up the funding for a business, reclaiming back taxes, quitting a costly dependency on caffeine or petrol, negotiating with a family member who thinks we've gone off our rockers. Act, Pressfield says, in the face of fear. Some things might be scary but we should do them anyway. David Cain, who wrote the foreword to *Escape Everything!*, also offers Resistance-destroying advice. He says we should periodically ask ourselves the question: 'Given my dreams and goals, what is honestly the smartest way to spend my next thirty minutes?' The answer probably isn't to have a cigarette, make a third cup of tea or completely revolutionise the filing of a record collection. To concoct and implement an escape plan, we do, unfortunately, have to show up. It'll pay off.

## ANXIETY

We're living in a culture of anxiety. In a way, it's a luxury, a 'first-world problem' as the people of the internet might put it. If we were tilling fields in medieval England or living through wartime hell, we might not have time for anxiety. As it stands, however, it's a problem in our culture.

I've always been a slightly nervous fellow myself and can attest to the fact that anxiety has no place in the good life. My nervousness has been detrimental in the past to making and keeping friends and to enjoying free time. As long as I can remember, I've experienced restlessness, twitches, pointless unease, fear of accidents. When I was little, I identified with Wade Duck from the *Orson's Farm* cartoon: he was afraid of both darkness and daylight and generally went around with an aura of neurosis. As a teenager, I identified with Woody Allen. As an adult, I've largely defeated the problem, partly by confronting a few token fears as a way of proving to myself that even worst case scenarios can be dealt with rationally; by tricking myself into identifying with calm and stoical figures in the hopes that their attitudes might rub off on me; and by learning to accept that a general level of background nervousness is both normal and tolerable. Doubtless there are more thorough ways of dealing with anxiety through meditation, psychotherapy or pharmaceutical intervention, but my own little techniques seem to work for me. Besides, a nervous disposition makes scary movies better value for money.

Anxiety is a barrier to the good life. It is corrosive to our health, physical and mental. It detracts from our enjoyment of free time. It stops us from appreciating our environment. It reduces what sensory pleasure we might take in. It prevents us from speaking confidently in public, even when we know we're right and that our contribution is valuable. It inhibits flow. It contaminates our creative output. It can get in the way of maintaining a dignified living space (or else it raises the bar impossibly high, condemning us to a life of constant fretting over domestic minutiae). If our nervousness is interpreted by others as social awkwardness or aloofness, it can make friendships hard to maintain. Anxiety prompts bad habits (nail-biting, teeth-grinding, secret rituals), saps our will power for forming good habits, and can lead to dependencies. It can make us prone to secrecy or extreme introversion.

The culture inside The Trap does not help us to be calm, rational or collected. As long as we have a culture of bigger, faster, stronger, it will always feel as though we're heading towards some kind of singularity or fever pitch. Some say we live in a deliberately orchestrated anxiety culture and they might be right. Brian Dean runs a website at anxietyculture.com, offering nifty techniques for keeping a level head in the twenty-first century. He suggests that the causes of our anxiety are a combination of pointless work, rampant consumption, a corrupt and authoritative government and a shrill and manipulative media. That's the world of The Trap, baby.

A potentially modern anxiety is information anxiety, something Brian Dean writes about. The news makes us nervous. It highlights the world's doom and gloom, wars and atrocities: none of which we can do very much about. Since we're so helpless upon hearing about the latest atrocity committed by British and American armed forces overseas or about the latest affront to our civil liberties imposed on us by an authoritarian government, all we can do is internalise our rage and become anxious. That or leave an unpleasant comment on a website somewhere and further contribute to the anxiety climate. A common objection to news avoidance is that it's irresponsible, that it's our duty as citizens to keep up to date with current affairs. But when we can make no difference whatsoever, it's hard to see what the positive outcome of observing this duty could possibly be. It's a higher duty, I suggest, to stay healthy and in control of our personal faculties: to be able to function well and to remain critical; to protect ourselves from a state of perpetual shell shock instilled through fear, marketing and spin. This doesn't mean we shouldn't study political theory or learn about other nations, but let's do so through less hysterical channels than the party-specific politics and biased punditry of news media. If we really must read the news out of a sense of social obligation, let us do so infrequently, perhaps fortnightly, with dispassionate advocacy journalism. *The Economist* is not half bad. Daily or hourly news-feed checking, I feel, is best avoided.

The news paints an unreal portrait of a terrible world. Because it only discusses the very worst things, it often seems as if aeroplanes constantly fall out of the sky and that innocent people are being stabbed and shot and exploded left and right. In reality, crime is in decline and people are becoming more tolerant and liberal in their outlooks. Because of the media tendency to spotlight the cases of crime and terror, you'd never know it. Brian Dean made these observations as long ago as 1995: a Britain yet to experience rolling news, Twitter, internet news feeds, or ubiquitous info screens on buses and trains. The result is information anxiety: that we live with a surplus of negative information. The news is also salacious, giving us Page 3 girls alongside serious stories; encouraging us to rubberneck into the lives of murderers and their innocent victims; and to pry into the lives of celebrities on vacation.

Another type of anxiety magnified by living in a consumer economy is status anxiety. Alain de Botton wrote an excellent book, *Status Anxiety*, on the subject. Social status – one's perception of personal success or personal value in the world – has become so important that we live in a state of constant status assessment, which leads to a fear of losing that status or of that status not being high enough. 'High status,' writes de Botton, 'is thought by many (but freely admitted by few) to be one of the finest of earthly goods.' All too often, modern life seems little more than a battle for higher status: it often guides the decision to go to university or enter the workplace; it's what causes the scramble toward the most reputable universities and the higher echelons of a corporate hierarchy. It's what might cause us to choose a partner of high social standing over someone we truly love. (A strange thing about all this is that trophy partners, shallow consumer gestures, and pretentiousness are all such blatant indicators of one's being stricken with status anxiety that they're socially ridiculed. One must apparently find a status middle ground by simultaneously striving to keep up but affecting status nonchalance).

The way we consume and the ways in which we present ourselves are not derived from conformity or obedience, but from distinction and status. To fret about losing one's status or not having a high enough status in comparison to others, is the core of status anxiety.

A final form of anxiety relevant to this chapter is existential anxiety. It's generated by the kind of dread that might accompany the big questions of life, along the lines of 'Why am I here?' and 'How should I spend my life?' These are nerve-wracking questions, not least because we're too often ill-equipped to answer them but also because the potential answers are so numerous that we feel dizzy or blinded by the possibilities. If you feel anxious when trying to choose between the 12 varieties of pasta sauce in a supermarket, the million different lifestyle choices on offer more widely will be truly bewildering. This phenomenon is interesting because it offers a plausible explanation as to why so many people are content to become worker–consumers and to ignore the doubts that work and shopping are the highest states of being. Choosing the default path of the worker–consumer eternally avoids having to experience the existential anxiety that comes with asking the big questions. In a way, you'd have to be mad to seek freedom when life inside the Matrix is so soothing.

There is little external motivation to avoid anxiety. Nervous or fearful people are easier to control, to coax into sedation, to juice for cash, to misguide into making decisions that don't benefit them. It is easy to see that this would be appealing to people whose job is to maintain social order, to those who would not benefit from uprisings or mass political objection and to those who'd take advantage of us *en masse*. We can never be free from malign influence in a state of perpetual anxiety. In Chapter 12, we'll look at some techniques for escaping anxiety.

## OUR PERVERSE RELATIONSHIP WITH NOISE, STRESS AND BUSYNESS

Noise, stress and busyness are not advantageous to our cause. Aside from being immediately unpleasant in themselves, they corrode our health and impact upon the good life in a similar way to anxiety. They are tantamount to pollution. A strange thing about noise, stress and busyness is that they've become indicators of high status. To appear busy, stressed out, and to generate a lot of noise is perhaps the modern equivalent of being laden with jewels. After all, only a successful, important person is likely to be busy and stressed out and noisy. 'YOU'RE BUSTING MY BALLS!' bellows the boorish entrepreneur in the train's quiet coach by way of exhibiting busyness and the kind of high-level pressure she or he's under. This kind of behaviour has become a sign of affluence and success. So many people claim status points for looking like they're working hard. As my partner nicely puts it: 'it's like they want a prize for shovelling shit uphill'. (Yet oddly, the affluent busybodies have not observed that poor people are also likely to be busy and stressed out as they struggle to make ends meet. Are noise, stress and busyness actually a form of street attire: hoodies and tattoos for dullards?)

To luxuriate and to seek pleasure instead of pain does not seem to enter the modern scheme of things. Let's all run around like headless chickens and we'll never have to face the big questions, be accused of shirking, or lose our hard-won status as nut-crushing go-getters. If we build lives on a foundation of tranquillity and idleness, we may well benefit from a longer, more considered life but we might also face feelings of guilt that we're somehow not pulling our weight – that we're letting down the side in some way. This is a damning truth about our culture, that people are bored by or suspicious of Buddha and Epicurus but willing to celebrate and exonerate arseholes and busybodies like Mark Zuckerberg. The ongoing worship of noise, stress and busyness highlights the disparity between what we know intuitively makes a good life and what we actually do with our lives. Nobody sane would say that noise, stress or busyness are good, desirable things. Yet most people live with them every day. They even show off when they have a little of each.

Could it be that to demonstrate busyness is a way of getting around the 'service with a smile' demand of modern work? 'What we are forced into is not merely work,' writes Mark Fisher in the *Occupied Times*, 'now we are forced to act as if we want to work. Even if we want to work in a burger franchise, we have to prove that, like reality TV contestants, we really want it.' In a world where we're supposed to *want* to work, to smile as we're being exploited, affecting an air of ragged busyness might be the lesser of two evils.

## THE DESIRE TO COMPETE

Competition seems relevant in the consumer economy, where rewards are made to look finite. Everyone wants a piece of the action and the caveman brain worries there's not enough to go around. People blame Darwin for the idea that we should all compete, but this is unfair. I don't think Darwin ever suggested that the mysterious process responsible for giraffe neck length or finch beak shape also meant we should be dicks to each other in a mad trample to some imaginary 'top'. The idea of competition serves the purposes of The Trap. If we want to escape, we should forget about competition: we might compete with our own selves perhaps in a desire to become good at something, but not with other people.

A more sophisticated version of the survival-of-the-fittest theory of why people can be such grasping shits, suggests that the will to compete may well be innate but that it's manipulated by the masters of the consumer economy. Tom Hodgkinson in *How to Be Free* writes, 'If the slaves compete with each other, then there is no need for the masters to drive them on with physical force. It's so much easier. The chairmen of the board think it absolutely hilarious that their staff will work their guts out and compete with one another for low wages and with minimum supervision.' It does seem convenient that our struggle with one another results in so much money being spent and therefore funnelled up to the exploitative rich. Whether through accident or through deliberate engineering by the supporters of The Trap, a natural cause of competition can be found in the caveman brain's irrational fear of famine – 'irrational' because the caveman brain still thinks it lives in caveman times and has failed to notice the superabundance of the twenty-first century.

Beyond the evolutionary basis, competition results from primal economics. It's an example of what economists call collective action problems. These are perhaps best illustrated by 'the prisoner's dilemma'. Two bank robbers are arrested and interrogated in separate rooms. The first is offered freedom if he confesses to the crime and in doing so incriminates his partner. If he refuses to confess he risks going to jail, especially if his partner – who has most likely been made the same offer – chooses to confess. In other words, loyalty to his partner would make him a sucker. He has little choice but to betray him. Inevitably, each prisoner will betray the other in the exact same act of defence and both will go to jail.

The prisoner's dilemma happens everywhere and it explains competitive consumption. If Ian Stevens of Dudley Drive buys a cool car, his neighbours will be motivated to follow suit, not because they inherently love cool cars but because Ian Stevens's ostentatious acquisition has made them look bad. Competitive consumption is all too often *defensive* consumption. The best way out of this ridiculous cycle is to refuse to play the game, but as the prisoner's dilemma illustrates, this is easier said than done: to opt out is to be a sucker. The prisoner who is loyal to his partner goes to prison and the last man standing on Dudley Drive is left with a crap car. It's a trap.

There is, of course, still the issue of ego. I can be quite disgracefully vain. I don't mind admitting it, especially if it wins me some kind of attention. But, to my shame, vanity too often proves a barrier to my escape. My vanity manifests as a kind of 'showing off'. Some of this, I suppose, has been channelled productively into a creative output, but that feels like a post-event justification: my creative output would probably have happened without all the showing off and might well have been better without it. No. My vanity has got in the way of friendships, squandered free time, and resulted in occasional bouts of loneliness, unnecessary expense and status anxiety. Even today, I'll delight in seeing my name printed on the cover of a book or on a playbill, but I temper this pathetic behaviour by using a pseudonym. 'Robert Wringham' is so similar to my real name as to be barely a pseudonym at all, but it's unlikely to trigger familiarity in old school friends or former colleagues and, thus, I do not risk courting their approval.

I'm not alone, of course. Everyone has an ego. It's courted by consumerism and by the collective action problem that leads to interpersonal competition. Celebrity culture doesn't help either. It appeals to our vanity. It says 'maybe if you do something to get noticed, you'll enjoy the benefits of celebrity'. These benefits are not negligible: celebs are invited to high-profile, exclusive events; they're given free gifts from manufacturers seeking endorsement; they're given attention through fan mail and a boom of Twitter followers; and even hate mail has a lurid appeal inasmuch as 'the one thing worse than being talked about is not being talked about'. Celebrity tickles one's sense of worth. It is flattering. But here's the rub. Vanity and the pursuit of celebrity beyond a modicum of peer recognition results in status anxiety. If we're not famous or celebrated, we can experience status anxiety for what we do not have and run to peculiar lengths to achieve it. In the event that we *are* famous or celebrated, we live in fear of losing that status, much as a millionaire might fear poverty. Celebrity, as with other badges of distinction such as living in a hip neighbourhood or wearing a hat made of caviar, is a positional good.

Celebrities do have some value to society. Those justified in their status – inventive musicians, great thinkers – encourage the rest of us. Statues of politicians, philosophers and athletes inspire self-improvement: a conscientious tour of a city's statuary can prompt us to ask what, precisely, is commendable about the plinthed individual and what about them, if anything, is worth emulating. What elements of Socrates, Boadicea, Queen Victoria, Frank Sidebottom or Greyfriars Bobby are inspirational? What about them is lamentable?

As a wage slave in Glasgow, I'd sometimes sneak away at lunchtime to spend time in the presence of a small Buddha statue in the Kelvingrove Art Gallery, and sometimes a larger statue of King Robert of Sicily in the Botanic Gardens. Buddha is an obvious totem of calm, while King Robert is a somewhat hubristic figure who, according to his information board, was ejected from Heaven and 'forced to wear the robes of a jester, with only a monkey for a friend'. Both, in their ways, became useful role models to me. Perhaps we could all benefit from celebrity if we did away with vanity. Catholic saints are only canonised after death. Maybe it's possible to leave an inspiring legacy for the good of others without enduring the problem of vanity while alive.

Maybe we need some ego if we're to create. The key, I think, is in distinguishing individualism from personhood. Individualism is the personal brand, the aggressive competition with other egos in the hope that a lucky few will, in some way, win out. Personhood is the skill of villingly swimming with the other fishes but maintaining a sense of identity inside the crowd, both for our own satisfaction and as way of giving something to the others. We feel enriched in the company of, say Maya Angelou or Stephen Fry or Germaine Greer – people who've established a firm and jubilant personality – but not in the company of cold-hearted, individualist 'winners' like Jeff Bezos or Donald Trump. Consumer society can makes it hard to see the difference between personhood and individualism but it's a real distinction and can be a useful guide when we try to see it.

## DEPENDENCIES

Dependencies decrease freedom and corrode mindfulness. Judith Wright at softaddictions.com points out that we're too often suckers for shopping, telly gawping, smartphone jabbing, internet browsing and other seemingly benign activities that combine to detract from our well-being. Describing them as soft addictions is useful because without detracting from the seriousness of drug or alcohol 'hard' addictions it points out that consummate email checking is an addiction too. It's like going to your front door every five minutes just on the off chance that someone is there. It's a good example of unproductive repetitive behaviour that is not considered abnormal.

An important thing to strive for in life is *flow*: full unselfconscious absorption in a deliberately chosen activity. Soft addictions detract from our experience of flow and should systematically be removed from our lives. It's hard to experience flow when a shoulder demon makes perpetual demands for another cup of tea or a quick look at Facebook. As well as the big wheels of The Trap – work and consumption – these flow inhibitors need escaping too.

Another kind of dependency is what we might call 'subscriptions': the services and goods regularly piped into our lives. A magazine subscription is an example, but commitments to everyday commodities like razor blades, milk and toothpaste are subscriptions of a sort, as are regular events like a weekly cinema date or a Friday night dinner. In business, these subscriptions are called 'fixed overheads' but let's avoid business babble where we can. Once set, each subscription pours into life automatically. Wednesday morning is when the garbage goes out. Saturday night is taco night. Your favourite podcast blinks into existence at Monday lunchtime. The joy of this is we don't have to think very hard about how to spend our time: the week simply passes by, taking care of itself. You could run entirely according to policy or fixed traditions if you wanted to, never having to make a decision about what to do with your time on Earth today. We can't very well consider ourselves 'free' if 20 different subscriptions are pouring in, dictating how we spend our time. We wouldn't want to remove *every* commercial or social subscription but it's worth assessing every so often which ones are important and which should be knocked into oblivion. Let's allow our actions to result from decisions, not compulsions. The Trap would love us all to sit in one place with everything we need flowing into our bodies through a system of tubes and for money to flow out of our bank accounts in a similar, automatic fashion. Only in deliberation are we free.

# PART TWO

# FREEDOM

## IN WHICH WE LOOK FOR OTHER WAYS

Love laughs at locksmiths.
— Houdini

# THE GOOD LIFE

Look upon life as a pleasant voyage instead of a continual
struggle for existence and a survival of the fittest.
— Houdini

## HOW TO LIVE?

**I** have a dream. At least, I think I do. To be honest, the ideal I'm
about to describe sounds suspiciously like something from *Star
Trek* so it's not impossible that I fell asleep watching one of the
DVDs. I dream of a world in which work is no longer a reluctantly
attended nuisance filled with activities of the dreary, non-essential
variety and bookended by rotten commutes. I dream of a day when
work is an enjoyable, purposeful and wholly voluntary pursuit. I dream
of a day when shelter and basic sustenance are inalienable human rights
and nobody is forced into working against their will to pay for them.

The commonest objection to this usually comes in the form of 'but
who would sweep the streets?' I'm pretty certain this kind of objection
came up when slavery was abolished too. 'But who will shine my shoes?'
'But who will poach my morning Dodo egg?' There are other ways,
sir, I assure you. The objection assumes there's something inherently
worthless and unpleasant about the task of street sweeping – something nobody would do if not forced into it – a perspective bolstered
by the fact that it's currently a low-paid task, generally seen as menial.
In a world where we looked for true value in our work instead of
advancement and status, street sweeping and the likes would not be so

75

undesirable. It is, after all, a rather valuable contribution to the world. When not in Montreal, I live in Glasgow, where street sweepers – especially those on the Sunday morning Sauchiehall Street shift – should be given OBEs. (I'd say they should be given a ticker tape parade, but that would make them furious.) I asked earlier if it's possible for everyone to escape or if we need someone to stay inside The Trap, pulling the levers and turning the cranks. The answer, if this doesn't seem too much of a fudge, is that The Trap would no longer be a trap: yes, we need to clean the streets and mop the hospital floors but let us come to these activities willingly and as vocations or callings instead of poorly-paid and servile punishments.

Citizen's Income, to return to that momentarily, would help usher in the world I'm talking about: we'd all be financially able to refuse or walk away from dangerous, demeaning or poorly paid jobs. Minimum wage employers would have to up their game in terms of pay, hours and respect if anyone were to join the street sweeping team. People might come to street sweeping from a sense of duty or social contribution – just as many become nurses or soldiers or firefighters – if the threats of poverty and low social status were taken away. I'd be willing to sweep the streets for ten hours a week under those conditions, and few people are so ideologically opposed to working as I am.

When I talk to people in the pub about this dream, it's not the idealism that troubles them but a persistent concern that a life of 'pleasure without pain' is somehow meaningless or unrewarding. Without struggle or toil, they say, we'd become slovenly or atrophied and have nothing to live for. As someone who was once an excitable child who'd struggle with the emptiness of Sundays and bank holidays, I see what these people are getting at but the 'pleasure without pain' critique forgets that current modes of work *don't* instil the kind of 'pain' necessary to enjoy anything whatsoever: nobody watches the workplace clock mete out the moments, feeling grateful for how it'll magnify the sense of freedom brought by the weekend. Meanwhile, a meagre two-day weekend will all-too-easily fill with shopping, overindulgence and chores. The promised quality time, the real pleasure, never emerges.

If we ever see a job as a reason to live, it's probably because we're so bored that we've had to trick ourselves into seeing it as a kind of game – a game of promotions and pay rises, target hitting and time-wasting. Anyway, my dream is not that we engineer for ourselves a sort of mindless, untroubled bliss. Without work, it's natural that we'd come up with activities for ourselves. The 'pain' that people apparently need can come from striving toward something worthwhile: the studiousness required in learning a skill, the willpower and stamina of writing a book, or the dues paid in winning the respect of a community. Not that I believe this 'pain' is strictly necessary anyway.

When free and acting on our agency alone, we might strive to perfect our golf stroke, work our way through a canon of tricky literature, become experts in some small corner of cultural knowledge, learn a language, learn the names of the constellations, or work our way through the naughtier pages of the *Kama Sutra*. The possibilities are endless. Something approaching a career could present itself, but of its own volition and without your being hassled, bullied or shamed into it. Sometimes, just an interesting line in a book, or a curious point of view articulated in a film, or a casual conversation, can prompt entire projects. Essential jobs like street sweeping meanwhile, become less meaningless when we're no longer bullied into performing them: it might be necessary for some work to happen, but it shouldn't defy the human imagination to find ways of destigmatising those jobs and to stop filling those vacancies through brutal, economic force. That kind of work, along with nursing and childcare, would no longer be a part of The Trap: to be free is not necessarily to shirk social responsibility. My dream of a world free of meaningless, involuntary toil and filled instead with gently-arrived-at, self-initiated projects is a vision in the tradition of *the good life*.

'The good life' as a term comes from philosophy and refers to a vision of the best way to live: how to spend our time, how to relate to other people, what to strive for or dispense with. In Eastern philosophy the good life is of central concern: 'The only problem unconsciously assumed by all Chinese philosophers to be of any importance,' wrote a Chinese-American intellectual called Lin Yutang in 1937, 'is how shall we enjoy life, and who can best enjoy life.' In Western philosophy, it is important too, especially among the Classical and Hellenistic philosophers of ancient Greece.

Aristotle believed the good life – or *eudaimonia* as he called it – came down to living up to certain virtues. By 'virtues,' he referred to wholesome human attributes like courage and moral justice but also to less righteous assets like sense of humour, hospitality and good taste. Epicurus meanwhile saw *pleasure* as the highest good and that true pleasure didn't lie in work or consumerism. Epicurean values include the development of simple tastes, close companionship, freedom and to lead a considered life. These must be appealing values to the Escapologist and worth finding freedom for.

Aristotle saw his vision of the good life as wholly objective and that the job of philosophers was to arrive at an authoritative vision of the good life to suit everyone. This vision could then inform societal values, morals and laws. More recently, we've been sceptical of the 'perfectionist' vision, such as the one proposed by Aristotle, and generally accept that one person's idea of the good life will differ from that of another. The acceptance that the good life might be subjective hasn't stopped philosophy people and intellectuals from writing about it though, and independent good life visions hold more in common than one might immediately suppose. It's still possible to propose a vision of the good life without excluding anyone. That's what I'd like to do in this chapter, to help develop an idea or a character of Escapological freedom.

Until society changes to properly facilitate a good life for all, we have Escapology to get us there as individuals. It's something we can all achieve if we want to. It does not require huge bags of money. You don't have to be young, single, of a particularly privileged social group, or to have good teeth (trust me, I know). If the good life was achievable in ancient Greece, it's achievable now. Those guys didn't even have the BBC iPlayer to thrill them and we don't have Pythagoras slowing us down with his triangles.

## SUBMITTED FOR YOUR APPROVAL: THE TENETS OF THE GOOD LIFE

What is required for a pleasant life? After much thought, reading, experience and conversation with other Escapologists, I feel able to make some suggestions. In doing so, I'm guided by a particular ethic of Lin Yutang: 'No perfectionism, no straining after the unattainable, no postulating of the unknowable; but taking poor, mortal human nature as it is, how shall we organise our life that we can work peacefully, endure nobly and live happily?' These are my suggestions.

**Optimum health.** It would come perilously close to endorsing Maslow's Hierarchy of Human Needs (a rather old hat but oft parroted idea that material needs take priority over spiritual ones) if I were to suggest that health is first in a list of 'needs'. I don't. It's just one tenet I think is important to the good life, occurring neither before nor after the others. The good life is difficult to appreciate properly when we can't help but splutter and wheeze every time we go for a walk. To live without the background troubles of feeling tired, bloated, itchy, irritable or distressed will let us get on with enjoying things properly.

**As much free time as possible.** Nobody on their deathbed says 'I wish I spent more time at the office'. According to palliative nurse Bronnie Ware who wrote about precisely this, dying people tend to say 'I wish I'd had the courage to live a life true to myself, not the life others expected of me', and 'I wish I hadn't worked so hard'. This is why we need as much free time as possible and to make the most of it while it's happening: so that we might fill our days with activities meaningful to us – either planned or on a whim – or in a state of leisurely repose. 'We all agree,' writes Lin Yutang, 'that the busy self, occupied in our daily activities is not quite the real self. We have lost something in the mere pursuit of living.' I agree. Instead of hustling along and having our time filled by duty and by others, we should keep our time *free*. This doesn't mean one shouldn't play a role in the community, or fulfil a responsibility to family or sorority or friendships: but let us come to those of our own volition instead of being bullied into service by the threat of economic hardship or a loss of personal distinction. The idea of a 'pastime' as something to benignly whittle away the hours until we're next cattle-prodded into action by duty or contract misrepresents what our time is worth. The Trap gobbles up our time because our time is valuable to it. The Trap wants us to spend time tied to a desk or to a machine, obediently doing our work; or else tied to an expensive leisure appendage like a joystick, a shopping trolley or a tennis racket. It doesn't want us spending time in non-commercial ways, like watching the activities of ladybirds in the park or having a face-to-face conversation with someone we like.

Epicurus chose to retire, while still young, to the countryside with his friends. They wanted to leave behind the gossip, expense, subservience, materialism, and disconnection from nature that come with urban living. 'We must free ourselves from the prison of everyday life and politics,' he wrote. Now, I'm a committed urbanite, and I don't see myself voluntarily leaving the city for greener pastures any time soon, but we don't need to take Epicurus's advice to flee the city so literally. The real parable lies in his motivation for doing so: he wanted to maximise his free time. Away from the city, Epicurus and his chums would not need to spend time on politics or fashion or day jobs. Their self-engineered retreat bought them free time. The more free time we have, the more choice and mobility we enjoy. Free time is the very essence of freedom and precisely what we should want to maximise.

**A few dependable friendships.** 'I wish I'd stayed in touch with my friends,' was another of the common deathbed regrets recorded by Bronnie Ware. We all know instinctively that friendship is important but we too often let pride, work, family, money and laziness get in the way of nurturing friendships. Hence the commonality of that deathbed regret. We cannot enjoy life without friends. My friend Neil introduced me to the concept of 'the sulking ape'. Evolutionary psychologists noticed that there's sometimes a 'sulking ape' in chimpanzee and orang-utan communities, a simian who has gone completely against the grain and left society altogether. The result is he becomes ridden with lice, loses libido, and dies of a broken heart. In all primates, humans included, social interaction is essential for a good life.

As a gesture of friendship, Epicurus bought a plot of land, built upon it a house of his own design called 'the garden', and invited his friends to live in it with him. It was basically a commune like the ones that would become popular in the 1960s and 70s but he foresaw the problems of multiple occupancy living and valued the concept of privacy so he designed the house so that every friend living there had their own quarters for sleep, meditation and study, but also communal spaces for food preparation, eating, dancing and chat. The idea was to facilitate sociability and to maximise opportunities for encounters among friends. Epicurus's prescription is to value friendship but also to go, by present day standards, to quite extreme lengths to spend time – regular, habitual, non-ceremonial time – in their company. But is it so extreme? Many of us make a similar gesture today when we cohabit with a partner: when we love someone, we want to spend plenty of time with them, to share a bed, to share meals, to divide domestic responsibilities, to split the bills, to have regular contact. Is it a far stretch to extend a similar invitation to other kinds of friends?

At work, we spend a lot of time with people who categorically aren't our friends: perfectly decent people in all likelihood, but people who've been forced to spend time with us through economic necessity and selected by a corporate recruitment policy. This is directly the opposite to what Epicurus suggests for us, and it's not hard to see that spending so much time with people we do not love (and so much away from people whom we do) contributes to our modern misery.

We don't need a million friends. We *can't* have a million friends. Not effectively anyway. Too wide a definition of friendship seems to devalue it. When we receive a Facebook request from someone with over a thousand 'friends', we know he's unlikely to value our companionship. Conversely, too tight a definition puts too much weight on the shoulders of the people we do consider friends, and excludes us from a wider range of meaningful social experiences. We should focus, I'd say, on a band of good companions and nurture those relationships to the best of our ability. We should travel to see them, make efforts to call or write to them instead of just liking their posts. Let's switch off our phones or tellies when they're around. Let's nurture these relationships the best we can.

**An appreciation of our existing surroundings.** Perhaps the most important lesson from Epicurus is that pleasure can be found almost anywhere if we find ways to savour the commonplace. Better than buying commercial pleasure with money, he suggests we find pleasure in simple things, to cultivate simple tastes. Epicurus himself led a remarkably simple life. He chose to drink water over wine, clothed himself simply, owned little, and occupied a dignified but humble living space. For food, he had an appetite for the simple fare of vegetables, olives, rustic bread and cheese. Yet he saw maximum pleasure as the ultimate goal in life and, to this end, urges us to reject rampant consumption and to appreciate the things that come easily. Do this, he says, and we'll always be happy: no stressful trips to the mall required, no dependencies, no debts, no eternal hankering after the expensive or the exotic. In this scheme, pleasure will be commonplace and ever-present instead of aspirational and eternally elsewhere.

Contemporary to the Epicureans were the Stoics, a school of philosophy founded by a philosopher called Zeno and perhaps best represented by Marcus Aurelius (an introspective Roman emperor) and Seneca (whose maxims feel extremely relevant today and are often seen salt-and-peppering books of self-help). The Stoics believed that the good life was to live in step with nature and, like Epicurus, that simple living was the path to the greatest happiness or a state of *eudaimonia*. But where the Epicureans focused on the pursuit of pleasure, the Stoics advocated self-control and fortitude as a means of overcoming suffering and destructive emotions. It's probably not as much fun as Epicurean-ism but there's a lot of wisdom in Stoicism applicable to the present day, not least their practice of 'voluntary discomfort'. Just as I tend to sweat through a Montreal summer without air conditioning, the occasional exercise of voluntary discomfort helps us appreciate comfort when we have it, makes us more tolerant, leads us to be less dependent on luxury or perfection. It makes us appreciate small luxuries wherever they are, and to take little for granted, which is what the Epicureans intended with their simplicity tenet. When you're accustomed to drinking tap water, the odd glass of wine is a wonderful treat. If the way you usually get around is by walking, a rare jaunt in a taxi is an adventure that never gets old. The practice is also humbling: why *should* I have the newest, hippest and most expensive of everything? Who am I, the King of Siam?

Daniel Haybron – author of *Happiness: A Very Short Introduction* – posits that 'appreciators' lead better lives than 'consumers'. Consumers, he says, are the people who show up at a beautiful North American lakeside community, blaze a couple of laps in a speedboat and then complain about how there's nothing to do for the rest of the weekend. Appreciators, meanwhile, are those content to size up the new place, savour the new sensory data, listen to the birdsong, and sit for quiet hours at the lakeside watching the darting minnows or meditatively poking at a campfire. 'I wish I'd let myself be happier,' is one of the deathbed regrets recorded by Bronnie Ware, and perhaps we could be happier if we took stock and appreciated what's there already, to be an 'appreciator' instead of a 'consumer'.

Something I've learned from my habitual walking in cities is that there are a million things to appreciate on a normal street. The experience can be heightened by learning a little about natural history, architecture, behavioural psychology, astronomy, weather patterns. A few authors in the last few years have appreciated this fact and released books expounding on these ideas: Lyanda Lynn Haupt wrote *The Urban Bestiary* to help the city dweller appreciate the antics of pigeons, crows, squirrels and other city wildlife. Gavin Pretor-Piney wrote *The Cloudspotter's Guide* to expound upon the pleasures of craning one's neck. Adrian Searle compiled *Look Up Glasgow* to encourage his fellow Glaswegians to admire the statuary and masonry of the city rooftops. Many who live in cities with light-polluted skies often don't bother to look up and to consider the stars, but even one star peeking through the light haze is worthy of our consideration. It seems as though stars have nothing to do with modern earthly affairs, but that's precisely why they're important: the stars, ancient and celestial, exist beyond the tedious modern concerns of the consumer economy. There's little as romantic or intellectually liberating as contemplating the night sky.

We don't have to flee to foreign climes to find pleasure. It's everywhere. We shouldn't rule out international travel, for it's a great pleasure in its own right, but appreciating our immediate surroundings – taking note of the things around us – is a sure-fire way to increase happiness, respect for our environment, and to find the kind of meaning and pleasure necessary for a good life and not offered by the life inside The Trap.

**Sensual pleasure.** Sleep, sex, music, the release of endorphins during exercise, the feeling of repleteness after a meal, the sensation of cool cotton sheets on a bed. Some of the best things in life are about inputting sensory data and enjoying it. They don't have to be complex. Some people go to extraordinary lengths to find rare sensory sensations, such as the characters in Adam Gollner's book *The Fruit Hunters*, who travel to the ends of the Earth to find exotic fruits. More power to them, but how can one possibly hope to best the simple sensations of a lawn beneath bare feet? Life without sensory pleasures – one of total abstention – would probably not be worth living. Inside The Trap, office life does not encourage sensory pleasure. A long and leisurely lunch is frowned upon in favour of a furtive nibble at the desk. Where possible, we should take time to do simple things – to eat lunch or to look at the stars and clouds – to their fullest. In the good life, we would savour everything.

For maximum effect, sensory pleasures should be sought for their innate properties. A nap, a social encounter, a meal, should ideally not be used for economic advantage, nor should they be hurried because of economic imperative, as with the furtive desk lunch. It might be difficult to find time to completely enjoy a single sensory pleasure (can every cup of tea be part of an elaborate Asian tea ritual?) but if we train ourselves to appreciate something like a glass of water or beer, to enter a state of mindfulness when enjoying something, to become a Haybronian 'appreciator' rather than a consumer, it is possible to do so without vast stretches of time or investment of willpower. Let us make it a standard part of our operational machinery. I sometimes play a game called 'the last piece of chocolate in the universe'. If I have a piece of chocolate, I sometimes imagine I'm the last human alive, drifting through space in a little ship after the destruction of the Earth. I have limited food supplies and, in particular, I'm down to the last piece of chocolate. Given I'm the last human and the Earth has been destroyed, this is probably the last piece of chocolate in the whole universe. I must savour it. Savouring is perhaps not a universally applicable tenet of the good life but seeking sensory pleasure certainly is. Epicurus said so. But how much pleasure is too much? The rule of thumb, I'd say, is that you've had too much pleasure when your pleasure-seeking behaviour has begun to inhibit other tenets of the good life. If obesity prevents one from obtaining optimum health, it may be time to stop savouring lard for a while. If sex or alcohol or outlandish comfort become addictions or dependencies and therefore threats to one's mobility or free time, one has a problem. But until then, let us take pleasure.

**Purposeful and purposeless intellectual stimulation.** Reading is important. It's not primarily escapism (though it can be, and there's nothing wrong with some of that in good measure) and it's not primarily a way of passing the time. Reading is important to the good life because it stokes the furnaces of our intellect, allows us to expand our understanding of the universe, both inner and outer, for practical gain and simple pleasure. It can induce awe, inspire respect, excite, piss off, and intrigue. These are things that make life worth living. They're the antitheses to the soul-destroying pen-pushing, tedium and loneliness that come with the consumer economy of The Trap. One doesn't need a specialty, as in academia, but can read around any field. We can be autodidacts. Curiosity is one of the best things in the world. Here's a quotation from the *QI* website: 'We are hard-wired for curiosity: it is innate – a fierce need – and, unlike the [other primal drives for food, sex and shelter], it is what makes us uniquely human. But pure curiosity, completely standard in children under seven and found in great artists, scientists and explorers, is, for some reason, quickly suppressed, sublimated or shrunken in most people. We make do with crossword puzzles, gossip, football results, pub quizzes and Jerry Springer.'

Epicurus was a supporter of the considered life: one of internally focused as well as outward curiosity. He believed that taking time to process our worries, ambitions, ideas, hopes and fears would provide a gateway to happiness. Today his advice seems obvious because we live in a post-Freud world and take it for granted that the repression of feelings leads to unhappiness. We tend to assume this kind of repressive unhappiness leads to stress, insomnia, and fidgety distraction. We understand today that the simple act of writing down our problems in a journal, talking them over with a pal, expressing them through an art or craft, or unloading them onto a professional counsellor, is psychologically helpful. Epicurus suggested we divorce ourselves wherever possible from the busy, urban world and to find the time to sit quietly and contemplatively to order our thoughts.

Intellectual stimulation can be either purposeful or purposeless, purposeful when we follow a theory or grapple deliberately with a particular idea or want to educate ourselves for some specific practical end, and purposeless when we simply want to experience the pleasure of submerging ourselves in literature or of spending time with someone else's wonderful, baffling, offensive, delightful, intriguing, arousing ideas. The good life is not necessarily about *knowing stuff or being wise* but about rejoicing in our ignorance, and enjoying the never-ending pleasure of satisfying its curiosity.

**A satisfying creative output in which we have personal pride.** It doesn't have to be the Sistine Chapel or the canals of Venice, but a creative output works wonders for the soul. Our creative energy – our *eros* – ought to be spent somewhere to avoid frustration, to give meaning, and to elicit personal pride. When we've successfully executed something we're happy with, we can stand back and know we've accomplished something meaningful to you. We shouldn't worry too much about how the critics receive it. We should just do our best and *know* that we've done our best. At some point in the 1990s, there was a TV advert for a brand of emulsion paint. It involved a man painting his house, standing back to take in the finished job and saying, 'I did that'. I remember my dad enjoying the sentiment and telling me to pay attention to it. Being a precocious little shit I probably snorted in disdain at my father's homespun wisdom but he (and the marketing people at Dulux paints) had a good point. The pleasure of doing a worthwhile job – ideally a self-initiated one – and saying 'I did that' is a good one. Whether painting a house, drawing pictures, writing a *haiku* or growing *bonsai* trees, a creative output in which we can take personal pride should be top of our list of things to do in the good life.

**A clean and dignified living space.** Lifestyle choices could have us living anywhere: a city apartment, a massive house, a boat, a cabin in the woods, a remote lighthouse. The important thing, I'm fairly convinced, is that such places be both clean and dignified. To deal with cleanliness first, one needs only visualise the alternative: nobody wants to live in filth and squalor. I've occasionally enjoyed a telly programme called *Hoarders* in which people with hoarding problems come to terms with their condition and work with a psychotherapist and a cleaning company to excavate the piles of refuse in which they've cocooned themselves. A similar show is called *How Clean is Your House?* in which a pair of chiding dominatrices ridicule the homes of slobs and show them how to clean their shit-caked toilet bowls or chisel cat puke out of a carpet. My enjoyment of this kind of programming comes from a bad place (a sense of superiority about not being a hoarder or a slob) and so I tend to avoid them lest it bring out the worst in me. But some merit can be found in how they allow us to visualise how we *don't* want to live. Dignity, beyond hygiene, is harder to define. Being forced into poverty through circumstance might feel undignified (and is one of the main fear mechanisms involved in making bold life choices) but *choosing* to live below the breadline in order to pursue things alien to the prevailing culture lets us claim dignity. At least in simple living, we can avoid the indignity of superabundance: is it dignified to live in a four-bedroom suburban castle furnished with crystal chandeliers while so many fellow humans struggle to make the rent?

**Some good habits to be proud of.** The benefits of building good habits into your daily routine cannot be understated. We are what we do, no matter how Bad Faith makes us feel otherwise. Intention doesn't count for as much as acting on that intention. If I want to be a writer, I must write frequently. Better still, I could work out some kind of metric to make that habit a fixture: write a thousand words per day, or write non-stop for two hours per day. If I want to be the kind of person who does press-ups, I must make sure to incorporate the habit of doing press-ups into my day: every morning, say, at ten. Habits are cumulative. If I write a thousand words per day and I'll have an 80,000-word book in the time it would take Phileas Fogg to circle the Earth. If I were to eat a pound of lard every morning, I'd be medically corpulent in the same time. This kind of discipline is different to the kind thrust upon us in The Trap: it's internally-generated and directly connected to what we *want* to do. It need not be connected to a commercial enterprise (though it could be) and does not need to conform to someone else's plans for us. I suppose the desire to build habits is a trick borrowed from The Trap, that doing the press-ups or writing the words is tantamount to punching the clock each morning, but I don't see the harm in repurposing that logic to serve us instead of The Trap. Are we now in service to some internal finger-wagging manager instead of an actual one? Maybe. It's something that troubles me slightly. But the key differences are the desirable, valuable output and the fact that we can, if we want to, stop.

Fostering habits can also help us budget our time and provide an idea of when to expect outputs. Malcolm Gladwell tells us in *The Tipping Point* that ten thousand hours of practice are required to master something. If it were a goal to master, say, the flute, then the habit of practising the flute for one hour each a day will have us master it after ten thousand days. A habit of two hours practice each day will have us master it in five thousand days. And so on. Committing to some good habits can contribute to a good life, partly in that we'll become good at what we practise and will be able to take pride in demonstrating our skills, but also because our good habits will provide evidence – to ourselves and to others – that it's possible to live well. If life is a system of habits, a system of good habits will, by definition, provide the structure and substance of a good life.

And there we have it. My tenets for the Escapological good life. Simple, simple, simple. Suspiciously simple? Some might smack of a 'real meaning of Christmas'-esque consolation prize but I've honestly found them to be true. They form the basic cable package upon which most people in Western society today will choose to build upon with optional extras or condemn outright as insubstantial or insufficient. The problem with optional extras, however, is that they don't usually contribute to the good life. Most of them detract from it. No matter how successful we are in life, we always come back to the tenets above. I suggest skipping that lifelong detour via status, money and stuff, and getting into the good life right away. My prescription for a good life is to keep things simple by adopting the tenets suggested above and ignoring the rest of the bumph.

If Keynes and his peers, those 1930s economists, felt we could have a job-free and Epicurean utopia by 2030, maybe we should start working towards it today by embracing the tenets outlined above. Why should we shrug our shoulders and say 'Keynes was wrong', when we can take it upon ourselves to fulfil his prophecy? We can do this by turning our backs individually on the work ethic and the maximum consumption ethic and by embracing the simple pleasures of the good life. The essay in which Keynes floated his optimistic prediction is called *Economic Possibilities for Our Grandchildren*. We can be Keynes's grandchildren if we want to be. Let us all adopt him as our honorary grandad.

# 6

# HOW ESCAPOLOGISTS USE THEIR FREEDOM

I have never been without some seeming marvel to pique
my curiosity and challenge my investigation.
— Houdini

## FREEDOM? NOW PLEASE!

Sometimes, an enterprising (or lazy) octopus will use its defensive
ink – containing, as it does, a cocktail of neurotransmitters – to
chemically delude a gang of crabs. The crabs have no idea they're
not free when in fact they're trapped in a sort of crustacean bliss bubble
and being, one by one, noshed. I daresay the crabs have a perfectly fine
time of it and probably aren't aware of their being duped, even on the
day they're selected by a tentacle and crammed into the octopod's eager
beak. I think humans are in a similar state when we're in The Trap. In
The Trap, we generally believe that we're free. For us, of course, it's not
a *complete* illusion: by some historical and international comparisons,
we are free. We're not usually forced into the army or a religion. We
typically choose our own partners and how we spend time with
them. We have hard-won social safety nets like welfare and social care.
Libraries and the internet provide access to largely uncensored
information, and while politics is dominated by the rich and powerful,
common decency at least forces them to deny it. We have astonishing
opportunities for liberty. But here's the strange thing: most of us don't

take advantage of it. We just can't be bothered somehow. There are few official rules to follow in terms of how we live, but we have a depressing tendency to buy too much property and work far too long. Few are satisfied with this arrangement but we accept it because of the prevailing idea – perhaps our equivalent of the hypnotic octopus ink – that this is the safest or most responsible use of a human life.

As residents of a fairly stable world in which the aforementioned freedoms are taken for granted, we have the power to create our own free time and to spend it – where legal and ethical – how we please. It need not even be difficult. With diligence and vision, you can do what you like. Rolf Potts in *Vagabonding*, a book about long-term travel, makes fun of Charlie Sheen's character in *Wall Street* whose ambition is to 'to make a bundle of cash before I'm 30, get out of this racket [and then] ride my motorcycle across China'. It's a charming ambition and one that many libertarians would enjoy, but as Potts points out, 'Sheen or anyone else could work for eight months as a *toilet cleaner* and have enough money to ride a motorcycle across China.' I'd also be interested to know what Sheen would do when he got to the other side of China with 50 years left to fill.

We all too often have this idea that we need to pay our dues somehow before we can go off and do what we want. This is what 'pie in the sky' means. The logic goes: I'll work hard today and have my reward tomorrow (i.e. never). The Escapologist says 'Pah!' to that, and 'I'll take my freedom now thanks, if it's all the same to you'. We also reserve the right to eat pudding for starters and breakfast for dinner. Anything's possible when you're an Escapologist.

An Escapologist is a person who has become aware of The Trap, who has considered its mechanisms, and has resolved to escape. But supposing her escape to be successful, what happens next? How do liberated people spend their windfall of time and increases in willpower, energy and agency? Well, they spend it however they choose. That's the whole point. But there are commonalities among those who've escaped and they help to build up a picture of freedom, of what's on offer should we rise to the challenge of escape. 'What would I do if I didn't go to work?' is a commonly asked question. It's asked in earnest by Escapologists and sarcastically by dullards. It's a useful question to ask when you're still employed in a crap job or living in a place you don't like, because it creates a theoretical future: one without the rush hour buses and perpetually ringing telephones and with almost infinite choice over how to spend one's time. 'What would I do if I didn't go to work?'

Luckily, I'm able to answer this question using *New Escapologist*. People have written accounts of their lives and their escapes for the magazine – exhilarating tales of derring-do – and I've solicited additional accounts via a reader survey and an open question on the blog. On the blog I appealed to Escapologists to help answer the freedom question. My plea to them: 'There are many ways of spending days, so let's show the world a few'. Escapologists can be rich or poor, have preferences for cities or the countryside, can be introverts or extroverts. We live in different places and in different ways. Those who've succeeded in getting the shackles off really are beasts of different stripes to each other. Broadly speaking though, Escapologists report using their freedom for dilettantism and play; charity and activism; family and friendship; and creative projects and entrepreneurship.

There's also a tendency toward a leisurely pace. For better or worse, the word 'pottering' comes up a lot. Even those who leave conventional jobs or careers to become artists, craftspeople or small business owners seem able to function without the kind of caffeinated workaholism and lunch-skipping we see elsewhere. I'm often sent photographs of people basking on beaches or lounging in cafes reading their *New Escapologist* and giving me the cheeky thumbs-up. 'Taking the rest of afternoon off,' they say, or 'Is 2pm too late for breakfast?' A reader called Zeniab says: 'One of the first things I will do when I don't have to work is throw out the alarm clock and sleep more.' I suppose there are moments when some of these lives, which we'll look into now, seem charmed, but it's not our intention to boast about them. I simply want to show how an Escapologist's life works in practice. Moreover, the lives arrived at by some Escapologists are not the lives everyone would choose – many would not have the temperament to join Martin in his garbage picking or Jacob in his higher echelon stock market investing – and freedom often comes with its own challenges, impoverishments, frustrations and trade-offs, as we'll see.

## DILETTANTISM AND PLAY

The reader survey suggests that Escapologists, when they're not actively plotting their escapes, will most likely be found walking, reading, cycling, listening to music, playing musical instruments, cooking, eating or boozing. Good to see it confirmed in hard, sexy data that Escapologists are essentially Epicureans. The quantitative data is backed up by stories and anecdotes sent to me by readers. Reader Briony says:

> Neither of us have had a proper job for some years. I am eight years a freewoman and my partner Mr B took his liberation nearly four years ago. Apart from family and household logistics (which are certainly less bother when you're not rushing about trying to squeeze them in around a job) we read, walk, play a lot of board games, garden, travel about on trains visiting friends and interesting places, swim in a near-by lake, learn Italian and meet up with a conversation group. We meditate with friends, make music, cook interesting food, and spend a few hours a week tending a small business that provides enough income to sustain a modest (by UK standards) lifestyle.

Paradise, no? I also like the 'by UK standards' she sneaks in. Perhaps a key to freedom – or at least an indicator of when we've arrived at freedom – is this kind of perspective. Just as we looked to history earlier to find perspective about the way we work in the modern world, we can look to geography for the kind of perspective we might need to know when we're well off. An income of, say, £12,000 might be small by UK standards, but pretty good internationally. We might not even have to think internationally: our income might look shoddy compared to a neighbour but respectable to someone in the next neighbourhood over.

She continues:

> Mr B is currently interested in geology and has an annoying heap of stones and books in the kitchen that he's investigating. At the moment I am learning upholstery through experimentation with a staple gun, YouTube and mostly free materials. I have big plans for a summer house furnished for comfy lounging and cocktails with palms and jazz records.

The enthusiasms for music, walking, reading and boozing detected by the reader survey hold up, but another key way of spending time reveals itself in dilettantism. Mainstream society wants us to be specialists: to learn more and more about less and less as we progress in a career or course of study. Division of labour requires us to be, specifically, a yoghurt manufacturer or a librarian or a car mechanic: seldom are we encouraged to be 'an upholsterer, chef, geologist and polyglot'. This truly is a great thing about freedom: we can allow ourselves to be generalists and be content to be amateurs. It's not usual for the homes of Escapologists to be littered with rocks, taxidermy, microscopes, cookbooks, staple guns and *bonsai* trees, and for those things to move over after a couple of years for new curiosities and the tools of new pastimes. Long live the cult of the amateur. Get into everything.

Briony finishes on this note: "We simply don't have time for jobs or benefit claiming. Only boring people are bored." This is something that comes up a lot: that there's no time for jobs or paperwork when you live freely. Good things fill the void. Some people find settling into retirement difficult at first, but many report sooner or later that they're so busy with leisure pursuits, playing with grandchildren or generally poking about in the kitchen or the shed that they can't see how they ever had time for work.

Reader and contributor Stevyn Colgyn is an elf. That is, he's a researcher for the Stephen Fry-fronted television series *QI*. Honestly, that's what they're called: elves. Colgers tells me that his perfect day, when not actually in London doing his elfing, is one of rural and Epicurean pleasures:

> I'm woken by the sound of the cockerel and, though I curse, it's no more annoying than the jabbering seagulls perched on the roof or the crooning pigeons in my fruit trees. The eggs for breakfast are still warm from the coop and they sizzle in the pan with bacon from a pig I once knew. The pig was pampered and well fed and, when his time came, he was honoured and respected by using every part of him: sausages and black puddings, hams and chops, cheeks and fillets, nothing was wasted. No supermarkets, no packaging, just good meat from an animal that lived a good life. I wander through the garden to my shed past ripening brambles and vines and raised beds pregnant with brassicas and squashes. Everything looks healthy. The shed is more glass than wood and light fills the room. I'm writing my next book in here and I have several paintings on the go. Every few hours I take a break and sip my tea as I watch squirrels and jays playing among the acorns. I'll finish at 5.30pm, take the dogs for a walk across the fields and farmland near my house and I'll use the time to think about the next chapter and which vegetables to pull from the ground for the evening meal. I

might even pop in to the pub for a pint of locally-brewed ale with friends on the way home. Or maybe take the long way home along the beach. I won't read a newspaper today. I won't watch the news. I may not even turn on my television. There's an ever-growing pile of unread books that I really should get through faster. It's my perfect day.

I'm an appalling city slicker myself but even I can appreciate that pastoral ideal. I love the moments of 'nothing-in-particularness': the watching of squirrels, the walking of dogs, the drinking of beer. The life of the freeperson is a combination of being and nothingness. We also see the creativity and dilettantism expected in an Escapological life-style: painting, writing, cultivation of food. We don't need conventional work to waste our time and we don't need the anxiety-producing distractions of newspapers or the babble machines. Reader Laura Henderson sums it up:

> If I felt like pottering in the cottage garden around my house, I'd do that. I'd pick up the oil paints that I laid aside years ago and take painting classes. I'd move to the next level with the genealogical research that I loved doing as a teenager. I'd rent a small furnished apartment on the island of Murano for a month and try to re-learn my glass working skills, long abandoned on the altar of making-a-living.

## CHARITY AND ACTIVISM

I've often wondered if Escapologists are bad citizens. Striking out on your own seems to involve a degree of turning your back on society. It certainly involves turning your back on some conventional societal mores. It's a slippery question to answer and one I'm only just getting around to understanding: we obviously don't *have* to be bad citizens because we could turn our whole lives over to activism or charity if we wanted to. It's just that in practice we often don't and many Escapologists have cottoned onto the fact that big changes, thanks to bureaucracy, are difficult or impossible to make. We've already chosen flight over fight. Laura Henderson says:

> I'd love to tell you that I'd spend all my time feeding the hungry or making the world a better place, but after spending a lifetime chasing a dollar, I can tell you that if I didn't have to work, I'd do exactly what I pleased. That is the definition of true wealth – doing what you want to do instead of what you have to do.

Is this a problem? My Escapologist wife, Samara, suggests that society is like a honeycomb in which each person is a single cell. Escapologists, by cultivating themselves, can become fully hexagonal cells. The idea is that we can only have a mutually supportive society if we each maximise our potential or as Wilde put it, 'the perfection of the soul within', and let the walls of our cells bump neatly against those of others. Individualism troubles me (though Samara, like Walt Whitman, points out that individualism is not the same thing as personhood and I'm inclined to agree) and we need society. Escapologists who go off to remote cabins in the woods tend to come back to society, tail between their legs, when they need medical attention or resources or friendship. If we need society, it's only proper that we build a social element into our escape plans. Some Escapologists have done so.

I recently decided to build a social element into mine by adopting a charity (a rainforest protection charity called Cool Earth) and by joining the Scottish Green Party and the Electoral Reform Society. I follow these bodies and help where I can. I am happy to give them some time. Time is something Escapologists have that worker–consumers do not. Escapologists don't sit in cramped buses for two hours per day. As such, we also have willpower because it hasn't been leached away during the daily struggle. It's easier to make principled stances as an Escapologist because you have the time, the willpower and a better-controlled personal environment. You're less likely to betray your principles when you have those things.

## FAMILY AND FRIENDSHIP

When facing the grim task of completing the 'activities and interests' section of a CV, there's an urge to put 'socialising with friends' but we don't put it because it feels trite and doesn't seem to have professional relevance. Well, we don't have to worry about that as Escapologists. Free people spend a lot of time with family and friends and we don't have to be bashful about saying so. It's one of the most common activities reported. Jon Ransom says:

> I spend all night in the pub with my homies. And then I go home and sleep with one or some of them.

Sabrina Holland says:

> I do everything with my family now. It won't last forever, of course, but my children are still young. I'm a stay-at-home mum, a home-schooler and a small business manager and wouldn't have it any other way. My partner is always by my side, running another business from home. Our work is now in tune with our personal values and none of us has to be away from the nest for long. My parents and my partner's parents come over sometimes and we're always able to take a break with them.

Ian Newton says:

> As soon as 6pm rolls around, I'm out of the door and on my
> way to the teahouse or the coffee shop or the brew pub to
> meet with all of my friends. Life without friendship is not
> worth having.

A criticism sometimes levelled at Escapology is that you can't
possibly have this kind of freedom if you've got children. They're too
much of a responsibility. I can understand this, as I'm not sure I'd be
able to relax or read much or work on my *opus* with a herd of stamped-
ing sprogs about the place, eating my chocolate and smoking my pipe
and singing naughty songs about various authority figures locked in a
lavatory. But there are some pretty solid examples of Escapologists
who've raised armies of infants while also enjoying their liberty. Tom
Hodgkinson who wrote an entire guidebook, *The Idle Parent*, to dispel
the myth of child rearing as an obstacle to a life of freedom. In the
manifesto contained within the book, Tom writes: '*We reject the idea
that parenting requires hard work. We pledge to leave our children alone.
We reject the rampant consumerism that invades children from the
moment they are born. We read them poetry and fantastic stories.*' He
actually makes parenting sound fun and a good way to spend one's
liberty. I may look into having my vasectomy reversed.

Briony the dilettante says:

> We both help out at our children's school (my partner runs
> a chess club and I listen to readers) and we also take our
> children out of school one or two afternoons a week under a
> flexischool arrangement.

A flexischool arrangement! How utterly great. As someone without
children, I rarely hear anything about how schools work these days.

When I was a school-going sproglet myself, I must confess to lamenting the amount of time lost to school. I loved primary school (The singing! The finger-painting! The readings of *Where the Wild Things Are*! It was like a glorious hippie commune. You could even take a nap in the book corner if you liked) but even then I occasionally found myself thinking 'I could be eating cakes at my Nan's house now or thrashing my sister at Hungry Hippos'. So three cheers for flexischool.

We received a great article for *New Escapologist* from Simeon Barry (another Escapologist who loves walking and hiking, incidentally) who lives a very free life with his young family, taking them with him on an extended world tour. It provided a very different sort of education for his children. It allowed him to pay more attention to them than if he'd been at home fretting over domestic tasks and professional anxieties. Life on the road, he says, can suit family life and child rearing rather well:

> My daughter has bathed with an elephant, eaten sticky rice, rode on a motorbike, done karaoke in Japan, learned Balinese dancing. My son's first word was *bebek*, which means 'duck' in Bahasa Indonesian.

Travel itself is a common interest among Escapologists. It's not true of everyone with free time (some prefer to sit still, which is a valuable option when you don't go to work any more or worry about pleasing too many people) but many like to travel. I count myself among them. I like to go on two trips a year. There's a strange belief that travel is prohibitively expensive for wage slaves let alone frugal Escapologists, but I've found it to be quite cheap if you organise everything yourself and do it on a shoestring. Stay in Airbnbs for a pittance, stay in hostels, camp in your own tent. An easyJet flight to Rome from London costs about £40: cut back on convenience food or taxi rides for a few weeks and see the Colosseum instead. When I worked in an office, I realised I could save £3 each time I took my own lunch to work instead of buying food from the nearby cafe. I added £3 to a rolling total every time I was organised enough to make a tuna sandwich before heading out to work. It eventually paid for four days in Berlin. This process felt deliciously like scooping out an escape tunnel with a spoon: slowly but surely and with liberty calling from the other side.

## CREATIVE PROJECTS AND ENTREPRENEURSHIP

A cartoonist called Glad Stork says:

> In real life I work in corporate middle management, surely one of the 'bullshit jobs' alluded to in Graeber's essay, but there's light at the end of the tunnel. I make good money and I save and invest like mad with the goal of quitting in the not-too-distant future. Once I quit my 9–5, I will 'work' full-time on creating things: funny things, sad things, beautiful things, profitable things, mediocre things, whatever I feel like creating.

The creative impulse is strong among the free, lending credence to Bob Black's idea that abolishing work wouldn't result in universal indolence. Interesting things can be accomplished when we're left to our own devices. We don't have to be bullied and cajoled into activity: it's a natural instinct. I like that Glad Stork makes allowance for 'mediocre' productions and doesn't aspire to necessarily touch the sky every bloody day. It's an important point: not everything has to be excellent or mould-breaking and we needn't be the best at everything (or indeed anything) we do. Sometimes, to create is enough. To be the world's worst artist is preferable to being the world's best quantity surveyor if the former is done through love and the latter through force.

One thing that troubles me is how the creative impulse, at least in my experience, is all too often used to maintain the free lifestyle, but that's still preferable to getting up at 7am each day and trudging off to the bus stop half-asleep and against every natural impulse in your body. Much of my own writing is done to make money either directly or in a round-about sort of way. Still, this need not necessarily be the case. One could make money elsewhere, perhaps through a part-time job, and keep the creative practice pure. In a better world, perhaps one with a Citizen's Income, we'd all be able to keep our creativity unmolested by the economic imperative.

Reader Arthur Guerrero says

> Every day I wake up excited and ready to learn new things. I work on my blog, read, write, think and promote it. If I had more money, I'd do the same thing but in different cities.

Imagine that. Waking up with a sense of enthusiasm about the day ahead. Only the free experience it. No alarm clock. No commitments. No need to rush breakfast or to grab some kind of protein shake or energy bar on the way out the door. None of that nonsense for Escapologists. You'll find us in our bathrobes, drinking top-notch espresso or a fishbowl of vitamin-rich mimosa well into the early afternoon, when we're ready to jump into our projects and activities wholeheartedly and without being cajoled.

Reader and contributor Drew Gagne left his job a year ago and has been exploring the business options. He says:

> Solo, I'd travel, read, hike and cycle. Not so hard-living as Thoreau, but along a similar line. Given my thoughts about the meaning of life, I'd say those activities are as valid as any other.

He's currently looking at the economics of setting up a coffee shop (coffee being a passion), and of building houses in Mexico (where he has family). Reader and contributor Shikha Dhawan quit her well-paid government job partly to maximise time for idling and travel, but also to set up a number of small businesses. She's now a yoga teacher and runs the world's first Escapological consultancy, showing others how to scale back and quit.

## DOWNSIDES, TRADE-OFFS AND SACRIFICES

I'm often asked if there are deprivations when turning one's back on consumerism and work. There are. But that's not quite the problem it might seem. After all, 'deprivation' is present in any choice. The Escapologist who deprives herself of designer clothes wins back the 15 hours per week required to pay for them. The consumer who chooses the designer clothes deprives herself of the 15 weekly hours. I'd choose the hours in this example: I'm not saying everyone should choose the hours but I do think it should be a conscious choice. The Trap robs us of the ability to make this conscious choice by positioning deprivation as a purely material phenomenon. The Trap requires us to deprive ourselves of time on a regular basis, but most of us don't notice it happening. In the free world, however, we can be sensitive to these choices and know how to make them in a more informed way. The Trap only lets us know about commodity deprivation because that's what it wants us to be aware of (fear of commodity deprivation keeps us working and shopping) but in fact there's always a trade-off. An Escapologist might deprive herself of certain goods but she's done it deliberately and will reap the benefits of that choice immediately in the form of time, of *existential substance*.

There are genuine challenges and downsides to life outside The Trap though. Let me tell you about 'The Curse of Escapology'. Abandon hope all ye, et cetera. When planning my escape, I had to wise up. If I was going to quit my job forever and elope to another country, I had to get serious about it. For about nine months – the standard-length gestation period – everything I did was geared toward the escape. I'd work hard at generating money through my day job and other means; concoct new measures of frugality so that I could save as much as possible for the income-free months ahead; use my job to learn new skills, ensuring that I'd be re-employable should things fall apart; maintain a bare minimum of material possessions so that I could exit swiftly when the opportunity finally arose; and work hard at accumulating the expensive and difficult-to-obtain documents required for my visa application. I'd dash home from work, draw the curtains against the Scottish dusk and concentrate on my grand project. I'd often be unable to sleep at night, exhilarated by the prospect of making a break for it and planning the best ways to exploit the next day's resources to further the endeavour. I don't think I've ever been so driven. Escape is one hell of an upper. Once the escape itself was over and the mission accomplished, it was difficult to end this way of thinking: to curb the ambition, the excited flightiness. I'd do my best to ignore it, to spend plenty of time reading in the park and watching the insects navigate the corners of my beach towel, but there'd always be an impatient synapse firing somewhere in my brain, telling me that things weren't moving fast enough, even though there was no longer anything in need of acceleration. I found it hard to return to the less urgent state I occupied before the escape plan. Sometimes, an escape-the-rat-race guru will write about 'filling the void': the idea that, once wage slavery is removed from life, people will struggle to fill their day. For me, the challenge was never in finding activities on which to spend the new-found time, but in changing the habits I'd developed in order to win this new-found time. I worried that I'd been irrevocably changed by the experience of escape.

Strangely, I'd even anticipated the curse. I first became aware of its effect one October when one of my assistants at the library asked if I had any plans for Halloween. It seemed an absurd suggestion: why would I do anything special for Halloween? There was an escape to make good! Yet only a couple of years previously, I had been *exactly* the sort of person to concoct elaborate Halloween plans. I'd once built a functioning robotic arm for a Borg costume at a *Star Trek* theme party. Something in me had changed. I kept telling myself that things would be different when I reached Montreal: there'd be time to relax and to have fun once I got there. But even then I was aware that this strange and frightening new drive would be hard to shake. Let this strange curse be known to all aspiring Escapologists! When we make it to the other side, we must not forget why we did it. Once escaped – and while escaping – we need to relax and enjoy the sunshine. Otherwise there's no point. Perhaps we can install a kind of crumple zone in advance: a sort of buffer at the end of the track upon which we'll be running so fast. I suggest a lengthy vacation –perhaps of a couple of months – followed by a new project.

Future Escapologists might also need to be aware of survivor's guilt. It's all well and good being free, but if our pals are still in The Trap they might not want freeing – even if we had the resources to help them, which we probably don't. There's also a sense of 'leisure guilt', which is something industrial society has done to us. *New Escapologist* contributor Drew Gagne says: 'Life without work means I spend my time thinking about how to contribute to my household, which is kind of sad and probably only because we're conditioned to think we need to be productive. I want to do something more value-added in terms of leisure.' Whether it's cultural or natural, most people, psychopaths excepted, don't like to think they're freeloading. Nobody wants to be a moocher. Even if we're paying our way financially, it can feel strange or immoral not to be sweating for it. We need to shun this way of thinking, but it's not necessarily easy.

One downside of my escape journey – and one that forces me to admit that not everyone will necessarily have the temperament for Escapology – is that it's admittedly a pain in the arse to keep starting over. I've back-and-forthed the Atlantic more times than a Blackpoll Warbler (a tiny bird I learned about on my naturalist kick who actually crosses the Atlantic as part of its migration route) and usually set up a new home each time. I like the richness of life brought by this, the excitement of a new start, but it's hard work and requires planning. Those in The Trap do not have to worry about this. Apparently, when he'd returned from his five-year mission on the *Beagle*, Darwin clung onto Britain like one of his pet barnacles would cling to a rock. I can see this in my own future, eventually tiring of all the adventure. But not just yet.

Creative or entrepreneurial work may not be as efficient as employment. We might have to put in considerably more hours than we would in a regular job. Writing this book, for example, has cost me a temporal fortune in terms of hours. The appeal of such projects is not necessarily to make money, but it would be dishonest to not mention the time and effort expended, the late nights and the worries about fruition and reception.

A certain willpower is required to go against the grain so consistently. Escapologists constantly have to make decisions that many do not. The Trap caters for most people's needs, but when we go it alone we have to think on our feet a little more. Escapologists have to choose freedom every day. We can go back into The Trap whenever we like by reporting to the jobcentre and saying the words 'I'm ready to return to work'. We have to choose not to do this and it requires willpower. It can also be difficult explaining yourself to other people sometimes. *New Escapologist* has not won the attention of mainstream culture enough for 'I'm an Escapologist, actually' to be met with much understanding. There's also the constant questioning from well-meaning family and friends, having to constantly explain our weird lifestyle. Sometimes this isn't even directly about Escapology but simply about displacement: I get very tired sometimes of answering questions about my Britishness to Canadians. We have to say goodbye to the feeling that everyone's behind us and championing our life choices, though, if you're drawn to Escapology, this probably doesn't trouble you too much: when you're satisfied by the way society has planned a destiny for you, you're unlikely to end up on the lam. It can be hard to be headstrong, but new groups of people – fellow escapees sometimes – will emerge in our lives, which is a lovely consolation.

When avoiding news media in the interests of sanity and no longer absorbing the water cooler banter at a workplace, one sometimes wonder what the hell people are talking about when it comes to pop culture. People had been listening to Taylor Swift for yonks before I so much as saw her photograph. I've still not heard her music and I'm not sure I could pick her out of a line-up. Friend Tim, who is of an Escapological bent, has been unconventional for long enough not to have heard of Colombo. When this became clear one night in the pub, a stranger came over from a nearby table and said 'I'm sorry, but did you say you'd never heard of Colombo?' I thought he was going to whisk us off somewhere for an emergency screening. All of this is fine, but it's worth knowing about in case it's the kind of deprivation you don't want to go in for.

Still. Dilettantism and play; charity and activism; family and friendship; creative projects and entrepreneurship. Freedom can be enjoyed in any number of ways. While there are commonalities running through the activities Escapologists have told me about, the bottom line is that you can spend it however you want. You don't have to spend it toiling in a cubicle if you don't want to and there's nothing noble or right or even normal about doing so. Fly free, my pretties, and rejoice in your liberty.

# 7

# A MONTREAL YEAR

That will do.
— Houdini in Montreal

I wrote this book in Montreal. I came five years ago to court the Canadian lady who'd eventually become my wife, but I stayed because Montreal has the added advantages of being pretty vibrant and skive-friendly. Ideal circumstances for an Escapologist! Bars are licensed to operate between 11am and 3am, which are coincidentally the very hours people tend to wake up and go to bed here. Not a huge amount of work happens in between those hours, though much falafel is gone to town upon.

Since the Montreal summer and winter have quite extreme weather conditions, life is somewhat dictated by the seasons. You can't very well go outdoors for more than 20 minutes in the winter, so you end up learning about cookery, novel writing and beer. You can't do much in the oppressive heat of summer, so you learn about floundering in a pair of pants on the side of a dormant volcano. Only in the clemency of spring and autumn can you realistically face production, so you learn to cram your annual moneymaking into five or six weeks. To illustrate how true this is, Montrealers all move house *on the same day*: July 1st being the only day where the conditions are right for anything so strenuous. By the time you read this book I'll have returned to the hefty tartan bosom of Scotland, but I'll still do my best to operate around a Montreal year. It's no bad schedule for an Escapologist.

## SRING: WALKING AND NATURE

I wake around eight o'clock. This is not a deliberate decision. It just so happens that the curtains in our bedroom don't fit the window properly and my sleep is disturbed when a beam of sunlight starts to cook my face. It's no bad time to rise though. It coincides with the time Samara must prepare for work (three days a week, she's an art consultant at a small gallery). I'm able to help out by brewing the coffee, making the bed and improvising my trademark operettas about it all. Samara goes off to work and I'm left holding the fort. After some bed making, washing up and a leisurely shower, I'm ready to start the day in earnest.

Spring is characterised by walking. I walk all year round but only in the spring and autumn do I do so truly for leisure. I find myself telling people about the virtues of walking again and again. The exercise keeps you fit; the rhythm and solitude flood your mind with ideas; the sights and sounds let you appreciate your environs; your very presence on the street populates the locale and makes it a better place for others to be. All around are wonders natural: animals, plants, clouds, moon and stars; and human-made: architecture, statues, memorials, 'desire paths, fashion, behaviour. None of this is witnessed when you go around in cars.

As Frédéric Gros writes in *A Philosophy of Walking*, '[T]here is the suspensive freedom that comes by walking, even a simple short stroll: throwing off the burden of cares, forgetting business for a time. You choose to leave the office behind, go out, stroll around, think about other things. With a longer excursion of several days, the process of self-liberation is accentuated: you escape the constraints of work, throw off the yoke of routine. But how could walking make you feel this freedom more than a long journey? [...] only walking manages to free us from our illusions about the essential.' Ideally, one should walk for leisure. Do it for its own sake, for no more reason than the pleasure of walking. Having no wallet to spoil the line of your outfit is a good thing, so walk without economic imperative wherever possible. A friend introduces me to a Latin phrase: *Solvitur ambulando*, meaning 'It is solved by walking'. Most things are. If I have a problem, I usually solve it by walking. Either I walk to get away from the problem directly or I walk as a way of mulling the problem over, eventually returning home with something like a solution.

The deeper parable of walking is that it's a low-tech and no-nonsense activity that only seems to produce benefits. You don't have to buy any special equipment. You produce no pollution. It keeps you fit and therefore out of the gym and the doctor's surgery. It keeps you happy, stimulated, and connected. And it gets you from A to B without having to buy a ticket or fill up a petrol tank.

Perhaps my favourite walk is to our local market. It's 45 minutes each way (the perfect length for a walk) and the return journey is toughened when laden down with a bag of vegetables, fruit and eggs. It's a fairly scenic urban walk and it also allows us to avoid buying much at supermarkets. I dislike supermarkets and prefer to give my custom directly to local farmers: fewer food miles, better produce, a more sensory and human experience and better value. A tray of 30 free-range eggs from our market costs the same as a carton of 12 supermarket eggs of dubious provenance. When I first began this walking-to-the-market exercise, I was concerned about the potential of breaking some eggs *en route* or that they'd spend 45 minutes unrefrigerated, but in some 30 or 40 walks I've broken just two eggs and none have spoiled.

Not everybody has time for schlepping to a farmers' market every week, but when you don't go to work, such missions are pleasures. It's also part of a more general resolution to buck the trend of 'bigger, louder, more violent'. I've taken a vow of 'lightness,' to avoid the strong forces: the big academies, the big corporations, the big institutions. Small is beautiful. Money spent at the market is money invested in my values instead of at the supermarket, the strong force of food distribution. To walk there and back is likewise a commitment to human muscle power over the violence of the internal combustion engine.

Naturalism (the art of observing nature, that is, not that of frequenting nude beaches) is another activity facilitated by the spring. This is a new development for me. My attitude towards the natural world has been one of fear, suspicion and mild disgust. I've always cared about the environment, but traditionally liked to keep it at a distance. My mate Dan once videoed me on his phone as I gingerly shuffled down a dirt bank on Mount Royal in wholly-impractical shoes: at one point in the video (he showed it to me immediately) I grab hold of a tree branch on which to steady myself, only to be visibly revolted by the soily mark it leaves on the palm of my hand. Watching the video and listening to Dan laughing at my revulsion to nature, I felt a profound sense of shame and I resolved to do better.

I began by reading the works of naturalists and soon fell in love with people like Gerald Durrell, Leonard Dubkin and Lyanda Lynn Haupt. Even Darwin's early nature writing proved accessible and rewarding. An absurd, pollution-breathing landlubber with a dearth of nature knowledge, I found within me a vacuum in need of filling. Natural history, it turns out, is more a kind of amateur observation than a strict science. Far from dry and scientific, the writings of naturalists lie somewhere between middlebrow travelogue and passionate memoir, usually written by avuncular men with the adventurous souls of children. Reading their work has helped me develop a sense of wonder about the natural world, where once there lay a vague sense of trepidation and distaste. A great, grey misery has left me, replaced with an airy sense of wonder. No mean feat. And now, I take nature walks, admiring the mosses and mushrooms and the birds and bugs. I can name many of them now. I have escaped the trap of urban lethargy.

I once saw a peregrine falcon drop suddenly from the sky, seizing upon a starling who'd been pecking around for morsels. Right in the city. Such spectacle cannot be bought and lacks a certain serendipity when seen on television. It's available just by going out into town. To see nature, one need not journey to some exotic location or even into the countryside if one does not so wish.

As well as a personal desire to overcome my rather pathetic floundering in nature, Natural history is worth doing in its own right. It is cheap, easy, gentle, can be done anywhere, does not necessarily require material accumulation and ought not to harm the environment or feed the capitalist machine.

In the evenings, if we've no other plans, I cook for us. We have a general policy of no work after seven o'clock in the evening so that we don't fall into the neo-liberal trap of grafting into the wee small hours. We don't obey this rule slavishly, but, generally speaking, it's pencils down at seven. After dinner, we might watch a film, usually something from the 1960s in which most of the stars are now dead or wrinkly. To unwind finally, I put my performance skills to use and read a chapter from a book until one of us conks out.

## SUMMER: STOICISM

I wake around nine o'clock, restful sleep extended by the pleasing white noise of an electric fan. I then lie there, sweltering. How, I wonder, can I possibly face the day? Only dehydration prompts me to leave the relative coolness of the bedroom. Montreal summers are oppressively hot. 27°C (80°F) is probably typical but, for a few weeks, temperatures rocket. If you're not defeated by the heat, the humidity gets you. The combination becomes almost intolerable and our main activity, we're eventually forced to concede, is simply to keep cool. You have little choice but to flop around like some kind of beached marine animal. Barely any work gets done and you end up with a month-long siesta. It's all you can do to try to enjoy the sunshine.

I spend most of my summer collapsed in a hammock on the balcony enjoying whatever breeze might come along. In doing so, I'm seldom alone: 17 storeys of neighbours will also be out there, reading, laptop-ping, smoking, cooking on barbecues. As I say, Montreal is very skive-friendly. Friends refuse to visit our apartment in the height of summer, for an air conditioning unit is fairly essential and we don't have one. Of course, the lack of air conditioning is a good opportunity to practise Stoicism.

The ancient school of Stoicism, as we saw earlier, concerned itself with the good life and concluded that tolerance to discomfort is the best way to face the world. This is possible by voluntarily practising discomfort. As the simulated virus in a flu shot inoculates you against influenza, some deliberately endured discomfort will help you to steel yourself against the real thing which, sooner or later, will come. I think there's wisdom in this. Putting up with the Montreal summer is best seen as an exercise in Stoicism. So I sweat it out.

The way I see it, if you can convince your body to survive in different terrains and climates, you'll be less dependent upon absurd levels of comfort. You will increase your potential: you won't say 'I can't' [work in a bakery/read in the hot park/visit Africa] because of heat. If you banish your intolerance to temperatures, weather conditions, heights, pollen, alien cultures, through adaptation, you'll be defeated by fewer things. There are strengths in Stoicism. In Montreal, I'm one of the 'mad dogs and Englishmen' who go out in the midday sun.

In summer, I feel like Robinson Crusoe: a lone Brit on an island, roaming the sun-blasted landscape in a pair of shorts and nothing else. I sometimes grow my hair and a scruff of a beard to complete the look. It's liberating to be free of my ego during these moments: I'm more nor-mally a dandy, wearing tailor-made suits and swanning around disdain-fully at parties. Permission is granted by the nihilism of heat to shun this and be Robinson Crusoe for a few months out of the year.

## AUTUMN: CREATIVITY AND MICROBREW

Autumn sees a return to hard work, though I do not usually mean very much harder than literary work. It's important to have a creative output capable of spiritual satisfaction and income generation. It's natural. Without getting too pagan about it, I think it comes from some sort of *erotic* desire, a kind of life-giving or creative urge. I've often wondered if a consumption/production imbalance is a common source of unhappiness or dissatisfaction. But perhaps the most important thing about creative output is that it gives *meaning*. I've never heard of an Escapologist who has fled all the bad things in life – work, debt, poverty, stress – but chooses to spend it living in squalor and playing video games. We're well within our rights to do so, of course: doing what we *want* is the whole point of Escapology, but it does seem that, after a while, the urge to act is great. Projects must be found if one's life is to be at all good. Writing is meaningful to me: for you it might be writing too, but equally (or additionally) it might be surfing, painting, bodging, millinery, tattooing.

Autumn is also a time for beer. The cooling weather and crunchy leaves underfoot prompt a certain medievalism in our dietary habits. Bread and beer reign supreme. Montreal is a good place for beer worship as almost any good bar here is also a microbrewery, brimming over with craft beers brewed on the premises. Microbrewed beer is more characterful, unlikely to be chemically-enhanced, is healthier, cheaper, stronger and tastier. Once again, small is beautiful. With a microbrew-style approach to any industry, we can escape the culture of 'bigger, louder, more violent'. Independence is freedom.

## WINTER: RETREAT

In winter, I rise as late as 11. If I'm lucky, the sky will be a slate, Victorian grey to remind me of Britain. If I'm unlucky, it'll still be dark. If lucky, I'll rise naturally, filled with dozy warmth. If unlucky, I'm woken by the racket of klaxons: a warning that someone's car is about to be towed to make way for snow shovellers. *Tow it!* I always think. *Just tow it!* Why should a whole city block of some thousand people be rattled awake by this horrible din because some idiot has left his car out?

With great expenditure of internal resources, I convince my stiff body to clamber out of bed. The heating will have dried my eyes into sticky little gumballs and my tongue will feel like a dusty leather bookmark.

Because of the snow and the astonishingly low temperatures (how can this be the same city that gives such scorching summers?) the activity of winter is total hibernation. Or at least *retreat*. 'You can't let it slow you down,' my local friend Chris once said, to which I can only reply, 'Are you out of your mind?' In winter, I venture outdoors as infrequently as possible. The mission is to stay warm. It's even a common expression in winter, used when parting company: instead of saying 'Goodbye,' you say, 'Stay Warm'.

Where the summer inspires me to become Robinson Crusoe, winter inspires me to be Scott of the Antarctic. I somehow held a part-time job in a science library one winter and I found the buses so unreliable that I took to walking 45 minutes each morning. It was a test of endurance to walk so far in temperatures as low as −30°C, especially for work of all things, but at least in walking hot blood will pump. The bus could easily be a half-hour late, and standing still at a bus stop for so long is intolerable and dangerous. So I walked. I visualised myself as Captain Scott, trudging one step at a time, through the Antarctic wastes, wind and snow blasting my face. My first order of duty when finally reaching the library was to retreat into the staff toilet, remove my multiple pairs of underwear, and to check that frostbite had not made the most terrible claim imaginable. Looking back, I'm not sure that job was worth it.

No, winter is best spent indoors and is most sensibly reserved for retreat. Thanks to these winters, cooking has become a pleasure. Preparing a decent vegetarian meal has become something I'm proud of. Cooking your own food is healthier than dining out and it saves money. Restaurants put a lot of salt in their food to make it more delicious and to win your further custom. At home, you can control precisely what goes into your body. I became a bit obsessed with nutritional science after reading a book called *Fantastic Voyage* by Ray Kurzweil and Terry Grossman in which the authors quite seriously posit that eating well and exercising might buy you enough time to reach a technological singularity, at which point there will be the facility for you to live forever. Whenever I eat now, issues of inflammation and fats and sugars and carcinogens are never far from my mind. It's no bad thing. It's quite interesting and it helps to stop you from dying. I don't really think I'll live forever with Doctors Kurzweil and Grossman but if acting in that way leaves you healthy and fit, then so be it. It's a secular version of Pascal's Wager.

The winter retreat is a good time for reading. Away from academia (the strong force of learning) one needn't specialise in any one kind of reading. Read it all. Be an autodidact. Slurp it up. The more widely we read, the wider our perspectives, and we'll be less likely to fall into the trap of thinking 'a mortgage is a perfectly good proposition' or 'perhaps working in advertising is a good idea' because we'll have a wider concept of 'normal'.

# MY ELEVENTH, TWELFTH, THIRTEENTH, AND FOURTEENTH JOBS

'ROBERT! *ROBERT! DID YOU SEE WHAT HAPPENED IN LONDON TODAY?*'

In my post-escape life I've occasionally accepted a short-term contract, often after having my attention drawn to it by a friend or a specialist agency. I accept a contract when I'm attracted to the work itself or when I've wanted extra money to fund something that lies beyond my usual tiny budget. Before escaping, I was a librarian by trade – still am really, and could always go back – and I love libraries. Unfortunately, head librarians are terrified of obsolescence and so borrow heavily from business, the leisure industry and retail, resulting in a lot of bullshit leaking into libraries from elsewhere. Despite my earnest attempts to campaign against this in my own workplaces and in librarian journals, the bullshit became too much. This, combined with the tendency of modern librarians to end up in strip-lit offices despite their deep and increasingly taboo love of old books, made me want out. In my time, however, I'd noticed two potentially self-saving things: firstly that libraries are everywhere (in places you wouldn't imagine: public and university libraries being just the tip of the iceberg) and secondly that there was a fairly healthy market for temporary contracts in libraries: projects frequently come up, like a need to move thousands of books in an orderly fashion from atrium to ventricle, or to manage a long-overdue upgrade of a digital archive from first to eighth genera-tion. Libraries won't hire permanent members of staff to deal with something like that, nor can they lean entirely on the existing staff. What's more, librarians are highly qualified specialists and there aren't many of us willing to show up to work for just a month like I was. I became a go-to guy for projects and cover. I can spend much of the year in repose and then breeze into a library, like Harvey Keitel in *Pulp*

*Fiction*, solve the problem, and then biff off again into the night with a glowing reference and a bag of money. I can stand to work when I'm there for a reason and when there's an end in sight. I highly recommend this freelance way of working. Not in libraries though. That's my turf.

In Montreal I took such a contract job in a science library. The library wasn't used by a huge number of people and I didn't have very much to do in the way of duties. I wanted money for a trip to Hawaii and I think I might have been hired simply because the boss liked to have 'an Englishman' around. I was given my own corner office with a computer, so I figured I could use it as a quiet place to write once my daily duties were over. Alas, it didn't quite work out that way. It was one of the noisiest libraries I've ever worked in and it was the staff who were noisy. Students and doctors would come up to me when I did a shift at the public desk and complain about all the bellowing.

'ROBERT!' my boss would shout from her office to mine, '*ROBERT! DID YOU SEE WHAT HAPPENED IN LONDON TODAY?*' After all, why pick up the phone or come round for a face-to-face chat when you can just shriek? You know, in a library: one of few places in the whole world where keeping the noise down is an essential part of the service. And why dwell on the work we all wanted to do when we could rattle on at length about events that happened 3,000 miles away, washed up on the shores of our consciousness through a Quebecois newspaper? A British soldier was in trouble in Afghanistan. Prince Charles was calling for action on climate change. *Downton Abbey* was being renewed for another season. If it was 'London', my boss wanted to know my take on it. I was, after all, her 'London' correspondent. Many Montrealers say 'London' when they think they've said 'England'. What they think of as 'England' is usually Britain. No amount of explaining the difference has ever helped me.

It went on like this for months. Political conversations shouted between plasterboard walls as people in white lab coats walked past and tutted. Houdini was defeated by a job in Montreal (it was in Montreal he suffered the blow to the stomach that later killed him in Detroit) and I sometimes wondered if it'd be the undoing of *me* too. But somehow I *liked* the Montreal job. For all its weirdness, I was glad I took it. It was arrived at voluntarily, which is why I mention it here. 'What would I do if I didn't have to go to work?' Sometimes, if it's not too absurd an answer, one goes to work. I went because I value libraries and like to work in them from time to time. (And also because I wanted to drink from a coconut on a Waikiki Beach and that would be expensive.) But when we're not economically bullied into work, when we arrive at it truly voluntarily, and when we know we can spend the rest of the year working on our art or lazing about, it can be pleasing and worthwhile. I never imagined Montreal – land of the 3pm breakfast – would teach me that.

## A GOOD LIFE?

My life doesn't cost much money. It's not filled with shopping or many other expensive activities. Overseas travel is one major indulgence but I usually only travel twice a year and I find ways to do it cheaply. My monthly general outgoings in Montreal are around 700 Canadian dollars: around £360. I realise this is extraordinarily cheap and might bear some scrutiny. Skip this paragraph if you're put to sleep by numbers. My outgoings are so small because of certain local economies, but also because of my tendency to violently shun consumerism. Here goes. Our rent is $900, which we split between us ($450). We typically spend $160 each for groceries ($40 each per week: vegetarianism is cheap!), and I personally spend about $90 on treats like beer in the pub. Heating is included in the rent (not unusual in Quebec). We have no children or pets. I never go shopping for leisure. My hobbies are mostly cost-free. I have no mobile phone, television, record player or car to spend money on. I no longer buy a transit pass, choosing instead to walk everywhere (though I do get the occasional $3 single ticket as a treat). The Quebec equivalent of Council Tax is probably Property Tax, from which renters are exempt. Our internet, electricity and phone line cost $28, $20, $26 respectively, all of which my wife sweetly covers as the wealthier partner (I make similar contributions when we live together in Scotland and local connections mean I become the money-bags). For me then, we arrive at $700. At the time of writing, that equates to £359.56. Two or three overseas journeys a year costs about $2,500 (£1,283), which leads me to calculate a monthly operating fund of $908 (£466). To put this into perspective, the average Canadian makes about $57,000 (£29,500) per year and even a 'non-earner' apparently takes home $29,000 (£14,500). I need less than $12,000 (£6,200) or as little as $8,400 (£4,300) if I were to decide not to travel.

I've found an efficient way to live and I'm trying to demonstrate what's possible through example. There's little point working hard every day in a job you despise in order to secure that glittering $57,000 (or even harder) when a perfectly decent life can be achieved on so much less. It's not for everyone. I understand that. For me, living without a mobile phone and a television are liberating but I know that some would struggle with this and would see such liberties as sacrifices. There's no point in being a martyr in the name of personal freedom: the key is finding the optimal outgoing and earning just a little bit more than is necessary to cover that.

Coming to Montreal gave me a lazy, beery, contemplative life and I fully intend to continue living in this way, even when I live in Scotland. You don't need to come to Montreal to live freely (though you certainly could do): we can do it wherever we are if we relax, live cheaply and reject the idea of a conventional career. Yes, certain economies I've experienced are specific to Montreal – fairly low rents, cheap electricity, no council tax for renters – but there are city-specific economies elsewhere too. Montreal is only cheap by comparison to Britain and America: there are many, many cheap and vibrant places to live. Berlin is a famously kind city to renters. Much of Asia is very cheap to live in. Even in the UK, there are economies to be found: groceries, for example, are cheaper in the UK than in Canada. It's a case of swings and roundabouts. If your city really is impractically expensive – I'm looking at you, London – one might consider moving. I understand that to completely relocate one's life is no trifle, but it may also be easier than one thinks. Money and stress saved on leaving the Big Smoke can be spent on travelling in occasionally to do business and to see friends and to marvel at the bright lights. I know for a fact that the bright lights of London and New York are easier to appreciate when you're not blinded by them daily. Beside, moving house is a good opportunity to minimise: there's nothing like packing everything into boxes to help us appreciate the physical burden of possessions.

I've escaped the world of 'bigger, louder, more violent' and the world of dull, mediocre worker–consumer wants like cars and full-time work and mortgages. Occasionally I think a smartphone might be useful but I talk myself out of it. I *never* think a car or a full-time job might be useful: they do not connect to my goals or values and would be a waste of my time, money and attention. Like Houdini, I've identified and studied the traps and escaped them. The result is a modest life, but one of pleasure and dignity. It is a life best symbolised by a library book, a spatula and a shoe. It's not much, but it's one vision of freedom and, hopefully, proof that it can be done. But *how* does one avoid work and consumption when they're so central to our culture? *How* does one enter the good life as we've defined it? The next part of the book seeks to answer that by revealing the escape routes.

# PART THREE

# ESCAPE ROUTES

## IN WHICH THE METHODS OF ESCAPE
## ARE REVEALED

Your freedom is achieved as follows.
— Houdini

# 8

# PREPARATION

*The public sees only the thrill of the accomplished trick;
they have no conception of the tortuous preliminary
self-training that was necessary to conquer fear.*
— Houdini

## INSIDE OUT

'I was five minutes late from lunch at the insurance company where I was working,' wrote poet Charles Simi, 'and my boss chewed me out for being irresponsible in front of 20 or 30 other drudges. I sat at my desk for a while, fuming, then I rose slowly, wrapped my scarf around my neck and put my gloves on in plain view of everybody, and walked out without looking back. I didn't have an overcoat and on the street it was snowing, but I felt giddy, deliriously happy at being free.'

Escape. There's nothing quite like it. I used to run home from the office sometimes – Pink Panther necktie blowing over my shoulder – because I was so eager to get on with fine-tuning my plans, crossing the date off the calendar and moving on to take the next step. There were immigration papers to deal with, investments to shunt around, possessions to list on eBay or otherwise slew off, a creative enterprise to cultivate and nurture. These were the projects and activities that *mattered*. The thing I was legging it from was both a prison and a threat. Remembering those days gets my heart racing. Emily Dickinson, another poet, wrote 'I never hear the word "Escape" / Without a quicker blood / A sudden expectation – / A flying attitude!' Doesn't that just sum it up? The breeze rushing through your hair as you pelt down the street, away from all you despise and into a world of your own creation or, even more thrilling, the great unknown.

The great unknown calls out to poets like Simi and Dickinson and me and you. 'There's no money in poetry,' admitted bohemian writer Robert Graves (whose 'Goodbye to All That' we took as a subtitle for *New Escapologist*), 'but there's no poetry in money either.' Sometimes we just have to do what's right and what's meaningful, money be damned. Escape is special in that, when you're doing it, you know you are *right*. A prisoner fleeing a chain gang while the supervisor is taking a whizz never looks back over his shoulder and thinks *maybe I should stay*. There are moral conundrums in life, times we're not sure if what we're doing is productive or useful or right. But escape? Ah, escape. By the time you've decided to flee, there's never a doubt in your mind. Liberty is unquestionably good.

An escape plan percolates within like a brilliant secret. It can sometimes feel like it's too much to contain, that it might burst out like a mad urge. I love the bit in *12 Monkeys* where Brad Pitt, imprisoned in an asylum, gets excited about the highly theoretical prospect of scarpering. As soon as it enters his mind he gets his arse out and starts bouncing on the bed and whooping. Alerted by the fuss, the guards come in. 'Sorry,' he says, 'I, I, I got a little agitated. The thought of, uh, escape had crossed my mind, and then suddenly – suddenly – *suddenly I felt like bending the fucking bars back, and ripping out the goddamn window frames and eating them – yes, eating them!*' We know how he feels. An escape plan is tantalising. The act of escape is thrilling. We don't even *have* to have a proper plan, it being entirely possible to just keep moving in a single direction until the petrol runs out or our shoes explode. But if we have a plan, we're less likely to end up dehydrated in the Australian outback like *The Inbetweeners* or frozen to the spot in Alaska like poor old Alexander Supertramp.

Escape plans are not concocted in perfect citadels outside society.

They're forged from inside The Trap. If we were outside, we wouldn't need to escape. It's obvious really, but it's worth explicitly meditating upon. Everything about The Trap – the consumer distractions, the fatigue after work – conspires to prevent our escape and it can seem like we'll never figure it out as long as we're inside, but inside The Trap is the *only* place we can plan a breakout. I know it seems like a trick of logic, but that's our secret advantage. Only prisoners have a chance of escape.

Inside The Trap, a workplace is a superb place to plot an escape. We can use those long, dull days productively by drawing up an escape plan. Most workers contemplate escape without even trying, though usually only as a flight-of-fancy, dreaming about a lottery win. The mind drifts in the direction of freedom. Where else? Drift with it. There's no need, however, to pin all hope on the national lottery or indeed any other unlikely rescue mission or *deus ex machina*. We can take action for ourselves by drawing up an escape plan on the company's headed notepaper. We can use the year planner in the front of a work diary to extrapolate an exit date and then cross off the days as they pass.

We can use workplace boredom as a motivator for escape. Keep a list of the specific things you hate about your job – idiot managers, fluorescent lighting that keeps flickering – as a further motivator, adding to it as you go along. Know that you'll say goodbye to all those things when you escape. Work gives you some time, a desk, hopefully with an internet connection: a useful tool in plotting an escape. Instead of using your desk and internet connection to play Minesweeper and gawp at Reddit, use it to educate yourself about investment and other jobs and other ways of living. You're also being paid to sit there, so you can even think of yourself a professional secret escape planner. Once you're out, you could make yourself a tee shirt or a plaque saying 'this escape was generously funded by _____ Industries'. Is it immoral to spend company time plotting an escape? After all, digging an escape tunnel probably isn't in your job description. So continue to do your job while you're there, but use the slack time that comes with the job to work on your escape plan: the time used by other employees to surreptitiously fart about on Facebook, read newspapers or smoke in the car park.

It is very pleasing to use a hated workplace as a base of Escapological operations. Money, motivation, time at a desk: just some of the useful resources kindly provided by a crap job. Already you're manipulating The Trap, teasing it into letting you out. Don't feel bad about using tools provided by The Trap. They're the only tools you have and that's not your fault. Any other tunnelling prisoner would dig with spoons from the prison canteen. Don't worry about it.

## JUJITSU

Just as we can use tools provided by The Trap to escape it, we can also use parts of The Trap against itself. As we saw in Part 1, The Trap has multiple components: work and consumption being the biggest of these interlocking wheels, while bureaucracy and our own terrified, stubborn brains are others. They're all connected, which is what gives The Trap its power, but it also suggests a weakness: *if we can manipulate one wheel, we will affect others*. For example, if we reject work entirely and don't earn anything, we'll be exempt from participating in consumption to any great extent and both wheels will grind to a halt. Likewise, and perhaps more appealing, if we steel ourselves against consumption by not spending much (in ways we'll discuss in Chapter 10), we can earn enough money through work to leave it. Once a certain sum is earned and saved or invested, we can walk out and never come back. Two load-bearing parts of The Trap will collapse in on themselves when used against each other.

Shunning or mastering bureaucracy (in ways we'll discuss in Chapter 11) will decrease our dependency on both work and consumption in that we'll no longer need employers or employees to negotiate bureaucracy for us. Likewise, mastering psychological foibles – like unfounded fear, anxiety and Resistance – will lead to a kind of personal sovereignty, a position from which we'll be bemused at how we ever went to work in the first place or ever bought a stupid piece of consumer tat we didn't need.

This interconnectedness of The Trap's key components is part of what keeps us ensnared, but once we see that interconnectedness as a design flaw, we can use it to our advantage. Armed with this knowledge, we must now perform two magic tricks: one to help us find courage and one to help to define our idea of freedom.

## FINDING COURAGE

Contemplating escape can be nerve-wracking. Like Houdini, we must find courage. Unlike the trick itself, which can be public and sensational, the finding of courage is a private feat. The best way to do this is to properly contemplate our fear. Self-helper, Tim Ferriss has a good technique for this. It's called 'Fear Setting'.

Imagine the absolute worst-case scenario that could result from your foolhardy escape plan and think about how you'd recover if it completely failed. You'd probably just go back to work in a similar job to the one you left, after a period of tedious job searching. This would be a defeat and a return to square one but it's not so terrible as worst case scenarios go. It wouldn't cost you a limb or your roguish good looks.

Maybe a return to work would involve starting on a lower rung of the corporate ladder to the one you left, but if you don't care about that ladder any more it doesn't matter very much. It'll cost you money in lost revenue, but you'd only have put that money in the bank or spent it on something daft anyway. You can always recover from a defeat and you'll have had fun in the process that led you there. If you have to return (which, hopefully, you won't) you'll at least have enjoyed some years of freedom (youthful, healthy, prime-of-your-life freedom) and will have some interesting tales of freedom and failure with which to regale your colleagues at the water cooler.

After sheepishly returning to the mundanity of The Trap for a while, one could even take the ride again. Let's be like Steve McQueen in *The Great Escape*, who flees the camp again and again only to be recaptured and comically returned to 'the cooler' each time. McQueen could have been killed in the process, something we probably don't have to worry about.

This fear setting exercise is useful, I think, and not a million miles from what the Stoics advised regarding the power of negative thinking. Before acting on an escape plan, we must ask ourselves honestly: what are we afraid of? Once we've blown away the fantasy and defined a realistic worst-case scenario, we can ask ourselves if we'd be able to face it. Of course we could. Would we be able to bounce back? Certainly. When we can look this problem in the eye without flinching, we're probably ready. All that frightened us in the first place was one of the weird, psychological distortions that sometimes happen inside The Trap. In reality, we have courage. We always did.

## DEFINE FREEDOM

In *Dandelion Wine*, Ray Bradbury's young protagonist lists some of his plans. 'See Istanbul,' he says, 'Port Said, Nairobi, Budapest. Write a book. Smoke too many cigarettes. Fall off a cliff but get caught in a tree halfway down. Get shot at a few times in a dark alley on a Moroccan midnight. Love a beautiful woman.' Not everyone has such specific or spicy plans but before using The Trap against itself, we must be able to say something along those lines. It's wise to know approximately where we're going before setting out to escape, to make sure we escape in the right direction. It's good, in fact, to conduct a *life audit*. You probably do this naturally and unconsciously already, but it pays to sit down and write it out longhand. I did mine in an airport lounge and continued it up in the sky (there's something about the transitional space of airports and planes that makes me want to take on the big personal questions). A life audit is a good way of taking stock and figuring out what we want to escape into. If your life audit results in a piece of literature as spicy and exciting as the Ray Bradbury excerpt then so much the better.

Occasionally, someone wise to the importance of this exercise will try and tell us about it, but we'll ignore them and carry on wasting our time on things that don't matter. Usually these people will have been on the brink of death before they've assessed their priorities. Old age or a cancer diagnosis or a car accident will have them concluding that careers and nice cars don't mean much in the long-term. I once worked in a cancer research library. Alongside the medical journals and self-help books on our shelves were the diaries of cancer survivors and those of people who'd been killed by cancer. That whole section of the library seemed to emanate sadness and people would never dawdle there. I read some of those books: the descriptions of cancer and cancer treatment were terrible to read but the worst thing was perhaps seeing how ill-prepared people are for the surprise that career and hard work and buying nice things don't matter. Time and again, the patients concluded that the important things in life are family, friendship, leisure, art, love, health, kindness. It's always a surprise and it's always poorly articulated, tainted by panic and anger. We shouldn't need the shock of a terminal diagnosis to realise this. We should assess our priorities by conducting this exercise sooner rather than later.

Jot down a list of five things you'd like to spend your life on. Five is perfect: more would be impractical, fewer would be to squander yourself. Rank them in order of priority. A list might look something like this:

1. A good relationship with my spouse and children
2. A rewarding creative practice
3. Frequent enjoyment of nature
4. A good relationship with my friends
5. Seeing the world

I'd suggest keeping your life audit a secret. This way, you'll not feel self-conscious about it, feel the need to show off, or be too selfless or righteous, and you'll never feel judged for (as in the above example) ranking friendship lower than your creative practice. Be completely honest. If seeing the world feels more important to you than nurturing a relationship with your partner, just write it down. Once you have something that looks like the above, treasure it. Consider carrying it around in your wallet, enshrine it in your diary. I'd not recommend laminating it though, in case you want to make changes to it later.

These items should not be targets. You do not need to make statements like 'I would like to earn one million pounds' or 'I would like to be recognised by the Turner Prize committee'. That sort of thing can come later if you're the sort of person who is motivated by targets. For now, just identify the areas of life you'd most like to exist in, and shuffle them around into approximate order of importance.

There's no need to be too practical either. Do not concern yourself with the economics of these situations. Don't think 'I can't include seeing the world, because it's too expensive'. It doesn't matter. Keep the list pure and we can worry about practicalities later. The exercise is about vision. Each item on the list should be *an end in itself*. Do not list anything primarily intended to facilitate other things. Money, for example, shouldn't feature on your list unless you love it innately. If you're tempted to put money on your list, ask why you want it. If it's to facilitate something else (for example, to buy a life-sized granite elephant) then that other thing (the granite elephant) is what you really mean to list.

Know that your life audit may not last forever. You might eventually decide that seeing the world is a folly and you're actually happiest at home. That will be fine. It can be useful to remember that you might feel differently one day. Know that you're not a slave to what comes out of your life audit. It is not a programme or a challenge, simply an honest list of priorities. Every so often, you'll be able to consult the life audit and have a think about whether your daily activities in any way facilitate it. You'll be able to ask yourself what needs to change in order to move more permanently into those areas. Will going to Uruguay for the weekend help in any of those areas? Will painting your toenails help? Will sponsoring a penguin help? It may do. But know how. When you're done and have a beautiful list of five things, you'll probably not be surprised to see that employment, rampant consumption, paperwork and anxiety do not appear on it. You'll want to escape those. But as if by magic you'll also have created a miniature environment to escape into. So let's do it.

# ESCAPE WORK

You will eventually encounter a committee who will bind
you so tightly that you will have to struggle for your
life, that is to say, for your freedom.
— Houdini

We must do away with the absolutely specious notion that
everybody has to earn a living. It is a fact today that one in
ten thousand of us can make a technological breakthrough
capable of supporting all the rest. The youth of today are
absolutely right in recognising this nonsense of earning a living.
We keep inventing jobs because of this false idea that everybody has to be employed at some kind of drudgery because,
according to Malthusian—Darwinian theory, he must justify his
right to exist. So we have inspectors of inspectors and people
making instruments for inspectors to inspect inspectors.
The true business of people should be to go
back to school and think about whatever it
was they were thinking about before
somebody came along and
told them they had to
earn a living.
— Buckminster Fuller

## ESCAPE ROUTES FOR THE CASUAL OR CAUTIOUS ESCAPOLOGIST

Working full-time does not contribute to the good life. It is more likely to detract from it. Clock-watching and strap-hanging aside, work's cardinal sin is its failure to contribute to the good life and the main reason to avoid it. It can, however, seem an unmovable problem. Without work, wouldn't we face poverty and social disapproval? These are the two fears that keep work such a central part of our lives. Until society abandons the destructive idea that work brings freedom (*Arbeit macht frei*!) and learns to be proud of non-commercial activity instead of embarrassed by it, there are more palatable ways to make money and win social approval than working full-time. Some are radical and some have been hiding in plain sight all along. I'll begin with some of these more obvious escapes and move on to the more radical. Starting with one cosy foot in The Trap and a tentative one in the land of Freedom will, I imagine, let us work up to the more outrageous suggestions. Here we go. Scream if you want to go faster.

**Adopt a staunch no-overtime policy.** If you have a job already, a good starting point might be to minimise the damage it does to you by limiting the hours it sucks up. You could begin by refusing overtime, working only the hours specified in your contract. Always, I'd say, take a proper lunch hour. A shorter lunch is permissible under this scheme if it allows you to clock off earlier in the afternoon, but the idea is to work the hours agreed to and no more. This is no radical escape, but it's a step in the right direction: the least you can do is work exclusively for money and never for the dubious merit of employee-of-the-month-style kudos. Sometimes there's a social pressure to overcome if the culture of your workplace considers overtime a standard sacrifice, but you have it in you to buck the trend. You're unlikely to get sacked for this and you may even be respected for your refusal to be screwed over. Your refusal to conform could be the catalyst needed to destroy the overtime culture: if you act confidently, others will join in. The liberty of the group can begin with the liberty of one.

**Part-time work.** The prevailing ideas about part-time work are that it can't finance an adequate lifestyle for the worker and that it can't get the job done for the employer. Neither is true. If we fortify ourselves against fad and fashion, ditch the cable television package and the thousand other drains on our resources, we probably don't need what is currently considered a full-time income. Moreover, if a worker spends less of her desk-time looking at Facebook or staring out of the window or generally feeling sorry for herself, she's also more likely to do a week's work in 15 hours instead of 35, so it's good for the employer too. Sadly, it can be difficult in some workplaces to convince a boss of the benefits of part-time work: it can feel a pain in the backside to them, to not have a team-member immediately accessible all week long, but there are arguments in favour of part-time work. If you're capable of doing your job in 25 hours instead of 35, your change in working practice will save the company money. Be flexible: agree to work additional (paid) hours in the event of a sudden crisis requiring all hands on deck, and agree to attend (again, for pay) any important meetings or events that fall outside the new hours you're proposing. It might help to have a good reason for wanting to work fewer hours too, as 'I just hate work and want to be free' might look like an insult or ingratitude: perhaps say you need the hours to run a burgeoning home business (ideally one that will enhance the skills you're bringing into your boss's company) or that it's simply more economically viable to work just three days per week (because you can minimise commuting expenses and/or limbo beneath a costly tax bracket). A compelling phrase is 'I can't afford not to' because it implies there's an economic necessity floating about somewhere, external to your ideals. If any further argument were needed, part-time work happens to be quite fashionable: it's on the rise in almost every economically developed country (with the notable exception of the United States). Lin Yutang, who writes in favour of a 'half-and-half' lifestyle or careful moderation, says we should look for balance in 'lying somewhere between action and inaction, between being led by the nose into a world of futile busyness and complete flight from a life of responsibilities, and that so far as we can discover with the help of all the philosophies of the world, this is the sanest and happiest ideal'. Perhaps we wouldn't want to escape work so badly if it only took 15 hours out of our week. Maybe it would even become a pleasure.

**Arrange a job-share.** In the event that 35 hours really are required to get the job done – staffing a public service desk or guarding the mouth of a cave – a job-share (a full-time job done by a two-person tag team) should not be impossible to arrange. There's often a reluctance on behalf of employers to allow job-shares because of the organisational challenge it can involve and the expense of recruiting another person, but there's also the benefit of two different minds working to the same end, bringing different skills and manners and ideas to the table. Two heads can be better than one and a job-share will lead to a more fertile base of ideas for the same investment in wages. Can an employer be so confident in her recruitment process that she's willing to invest all responsibility in one staff member? Why not minimise the risk and hire two people to do one job?

**Split responsibilities.** Maybe you cohabit with your partner. Suppose one of you goes to work, allowing the other to be free. Half of society would be freed overnight! Before the 1960s, a couple had a socially sanctioned division of duties. The father was the breadwinner, working for money. The mother was the housekeeper, managing the home and making it a pleasant place to live. A marriage was a partnership with a defined division of labour.

There's no good reason for the labour division to occur at the fault line of gender. Maybe 1950s mums didn't want to stay at home. Maybe 1950s fathers resented their sacrifice too. It also didn't help that we saw (and continue to see) domestic work as inferior to professional work. My recommendation is that we leave the gender roles in the dustbin of history but salvage the division of labour where both partners approve of it. This way, the money continues to flow and everyone has a nice clean house to live in. You could even *halve* the full-time job responsibilities if you liked: if you divide household duties equally and both go out to work for 15 hours each, your combined efforts will be the equivalent to one breadwinner and one home-maker.

In this gender-neutral version of the old breadwinner/homemaker relationship, same-sex couples would obviously enjoy the same benefits since gender's no longer a deciding factor in who does what. Come to think of it, a 'couple' need not even be romantically involved at all: two platonic flatmates could have precisely the same arrangement if they were comfortable with it. Symbiotic relationships take place in nature all the time: the fish who picks the harmful microorganisms out of sea anemones is in no way romantically involved with the anemone even if it provides its shelter.

Philosopher Joseph Heath looks at the problem of how society seems to value moneymaking as the prime objective and that domestic work is somehow secondary to that. How in this world, he asks, can we restore dignity to a stay-at-home partner? Personally, I think we should simply update our attitudes: we'll all feel better for it. But Heath suggests domestic partners double up as *artistic* partners. Artists, he says, can work on their paintings or novels at home while also doing the housework. It's not a *completely* unworkable idea, which is why I mention it here, but as anyone who writes books or takes painting seriously knows, the arts take time: as does running a home. Doing both is a big ask and the Escapologist will prefer a more leisurely pace of life. Better, I say, to start seeing domestic labour as equal to breadwinning. Don't worry if society doesn't see it this way: just do it yourself.

One of the good life tenets – the elements of a pleasant life – in Chapter 5 is to have a clean and dignified living space. By embracing the values of the good life instead of those of the consumer economy, we'll look upon domestic labour with pride. Domestic care is no longer a second-class duty but an important part of living. Whatever your gender, be proud to manage your home beautifully while automatically halving the toil required for your household to remain economically solvent.

**Temping.** If you're already resigned to a life of white-collar tedium, why not suffer in instalments? In a temporary job – a job in which the contract is for a fixed term and both the employer and employee understand that their relationship is not a death bond – one can work hard for six months, save half the wages, and then take the rest of the year off. Doing your job well and building a good relationship with a temping agency will help to ensure more work when you need it again. You could even add some high-flyer geo-arbitrage to the mix: work for a relatively well-paid temp job in Britain and spend your off-time somewhere cheap and pleasant in the Mediterranean.

A pleasing thing about temping (which I seem to be the only person to notice) is that you don't have to tell anyone outside your workplace that you're a temp. On paper – on your CV – you can make a chain of temp jobs look very much like a successful portfolio career, especially if you can give the impression of progression. You can do this by working in a similar field with each job and taking a slightly better (or at least better-sounding) one each time. Avoid the word 'temp' and portray yourself as a successful contractor, which in every sense, you are.

In employment law, temps are often considered self-employed. The reason for this is so employers can scam you out of holiday time and paid sickness, but it can work to your advantage too. You can also use the phrase 'successful completion of contract' on job application forms if they ask your reason for leaving your last job. It's certainly a better answer than 'I got frustrated and shot everyone' as far as employers are concerned.

One of the turning points in my old career as a librarian was learning about temp jobs. There was even an agency specialising in matching librarians, archivists and records managers with short-term contracts. When I'd started out, I wanted to become a proper librarian quite quickly and not to be stuck with the relatively technical and junior status of 'library assistant' for 20 years as some of my colleagues had. Libraries have only so many positions for qualified librarians, all of which are occupied by seasoned career librarians, and so the only way to the top was dead men's shoes. I felt, however, that a library was more likely to hire a young librarian if (a) the post was temporary and extant simply to fulfil a project or a maternity leave; and (b) if it looked like I had a successful portfolio career growing from 'library assistant' through to the duties of slightly more decorated positions like 'information officer' or 'information manager'. That's precisely what I did. I became a librarian just four years after leaving library school. Temp jobs can work in favour of the ambitious and career-minded young company man as well as the freewheeling Escapologist.

## ESCAPE ROUTES FOR THE RADICAL ESCAPOLOGIST

**The ERE model.** Jacob Lund Fisker, a one-time research scientist, has for several years been championing the concept of extreme early retirement. Philosophically anyone can 'retire' early simply by pushing away from their desk and silently walking out of the building never to be seen again. In fact, a quick piece in *The Onion* in 2015 had fun with this absurd temptation: 'Health Experts Recommend Standing Up At Desk, Leaving Office, Never Coming Back.' But if we want to continue living in relative comfort and having enough money to pay for healthy food and the occasional visit to the dentist, this won't do. We want to escape with our dignity as well as our time. The money problem, in other words, remains. Jacob Lund Fisker has solved the money problem.

His technique for leaving the rat race is quite simple. Take a job like everyone else but instead of spending all of your income immediately, find ways to save half or more of it, and then invest it wisely with an eye to long-term gains. Naturally, this will involve making personal economies and some careful self-education as to the nature of investing but essentially, through financial planning, you can buy yourself out of wage slavery. You can do so sooner that you might think. Jacob retired at 33.

A joy of Jacob's model is that it's so numerically robust. No other system of rat race escape works quite so well. By calculating how much money you need to live comfortably each year, multiplying it by the number of years you can reasonably expect to live (plus a safety margin), and securing that sum of money through earning and investing, you can predict quite precisely when you'll be able to escape your day job. You can then plan for this exit date accordingly. Why wait until the age of 65 to retire when you can use your brain to retire at 55, 44, or 33?

What's more, if you want to retire even earlier than your mathematically calculated exit date, you can either pump your money into higher-paying investments in order to increase the yield, or you can decrease your living expenses so that every pound saved can be invested in order to simultaneously lower the amount of money you need to retire on (because a lower fixed overhead means a smaller necessary retirement fund) and increase the dividend (because the additional money in your investment will result in a higher yield).

Encouraging yourself to think along these lines makes early retirement seem not only possible but reasonable. You can work out an escape date and keep it in mind. Print it out on a sheet of paper and pin it to the wall of your cubicle. Cross the days off your calendar until you reach it. Keep a countdown if you want to. If you hate your job and want to leave it, do all you can by cutting expenses and increasing income to bring that date closer to the present.

Jacob points out that the question of 'how much money do I need to retire?' is an extremely common one but it takes a rarer mind to think to ask 'how *little* money do I need to retire?' In other words, the less money you need to live on, the less money you'll need in the future and therefore the less money you'll need in the kitty to retire on. The less money you need for retirement, the sooner you'll be able to do it.

If your calculations tell you that you need £100,000 in order to retire in 20 years' time, see if you can cut back your expenses (or increase your investment income) by half and you'll be able to retire in 10 years instead. Cut back expenses (or increase income) by 75 per cent and retire in five years. That's quite startling to think about. How much do cars and games consoles mean to us? Enough to keep us in servitude for 15 years?

This 'freedom value' of economy is how Jacob – a person with a ruthlessly mathematical and logical mind – ends up talking so much about things like homemade laundry detergent, home-grown vegetables and home-brewed wine. Because he truly understands the value of a dollar, it's in his interests to lower his overheads as much as possible. A dollar to a consumer equals about 15 minutes of on-street parking or one-third of a latte; an investor sees the potential long-term income that the same dollar can generate; and someone lusting after early retirement sees that extra income as time detracted from her workplace servitude. If £30 can be saved per year by not buying commercial washing detergent, that's £30 that can be invested per year. If £30 per year can be made to result in a long-term investment revenue of £5,000 it could move your retirement date forward by a whole year. Nobody values laundry detergent so highly that they'd deliberately work for it for a whole year, but through negligence that's precisely what happens. It might be penny-pinching, but if a year of freedom is worth something to you, it might be worth taking this idea seriously.

And so this is how Jacob became an unlikely lifestyle guru. He'll not appreciate my describing him as such, but his book and website are full of information on topics like how to dress, what kind of neighbourhoods are best to live in, the benefits of finding a challenge. His website has a handy '21-day makeover' section: in 21 days (or at least 21 actions or commitments) you can enter his low-cost lifestyle by paying attention to where you live, how you live, who you live with, how you get around, how to manage your possessions and how to spend your time. Unusually for an economically based thesis, it encourages activities of low monetary cost and high spiritual gain. It is, to all intents and purposes, an *Ethics.* His way of living, arrived at economically, looks quite a lot like the Escapologist's map of the good life.

Everything you need to know about Jacob's plan is available for free at his blog, *Early Retirement Extreme* (ERE), and is expanded on in a 2010 book of the same name. There's also a well-attended forum attached to his website for successful and wannabe early retirees to post about their attempts to escape work by saving and investing.

**Create a 'muse'.** A tremendously cocky way to escape the daily grind is to create an automated business capable of generating income (precisely the amount you need to live comfortably) without your having to tend to business matters very much yourself. Such automated businesses involve identifying a niche market, finding a manufacturer with a product you can sell to your niche market, setting up a virtual shopfront and embarking upon a highly targeted online advertising campaign. All you're doing is matching a product with a market, and once your advertising campaign proves successful you can sit back and allow the process to continue on its own. It's like getting a plate spinning and checking occasionally to ensure momentum is being kept. An automated company takes a lot of time and an injection of cash to get started but, if successful, it will solve the money problem once and for all with very little in the way of pesky maintenance. Even if it takes a year to figure out, this is a better use of time than forty years of dreary employment. For advice on how to concoct an automated company, the best place to look is a book called *The 4-hour Workweek* by Timothy Ferris in which he describes such a self-operating machine as a 'muse'.

Using an online shopfront, a clever Google Ads campaign and a system of drop shipping desirable goods, you can theoretically sit back and watch the money roll in automatically. You end up with something like a Rube-Goldberg kinetic sculpture that takes money from online shoppers and tips it into your bank account.

Personally, I don't care for muses: it doesn't feel right to me to eschew consumerism while also surviving by it. It's a freeloading mentality wherein your liberty depends on the commercial exploitation of others. Still, it does work, and perhaps you can minimise your distaste for the muse by choosing a socially responsible product or one your core market can genuinely benefit from. Besides, Ferris himself points out that the object of the muse is not to save the world, but to save yourself, and maybe your liberty *could* be used to elevate the human spirit in some way (become an artist, give a portion of your free time to good causes) and it will at the very least increase the sum total of free souls in the world by precisely one.

**Become a cottage industry.** If the ethics of the muse don't appeal to you, or you can't be arsed with the hassle of setting it up, another long-term solution is to run your own cottage industry. I always hesitate to say 'small business' because the term is so depressingly dry but also because it's needlessly modest: a cottage industry has the potential for huge scope but will always be managed from your cosy centre of operations. Ricky Gervais describes himself as a cottage industry: from a small London office he wrote and sold something like fifty film and sitcom scripts, recorded and distributed the most downloaded and lucrative podcast in the world and made his way into the *Time 100* list of the world's most influential people. Whatever you think of Gervais's work, this is quite the organisational achievement for a portly comedian with a laptop.

In his 1973 economic treatise, *Small is Beautiful: A Study of Economics as if People Mattered*, E. F. Schumacher writes: 'The ideal from the point of view of the employer is to have output without employees, and the ideal from the point of view of the employee is to have income without employment.' There's a lot of truth here, hence the rift between the management and workers. Through cottage industry, it's possible to embrace both of Schumacher's ideals by quitting your job and setting up business alone. You can have output without the employees. You can have income without a job.

The somewhat glib advice to 'find what you enjoy and let money catch up with you' is understandably hard to accept by those who've been trapped in white-collar professions for a long time, but this is surely the best advice for someone starting a cottage industry: to what could you most stand to dedicate your time? What excites you?

Perhaps the most tempting route out of clerical servitude is self-employment. Many consider themselves successful escapees if they've ceased to work for someone else in favour of working for themselves. This involves a lot of hard work and instead of employers, you're usually dependent on clients. You can also find yourself in a position of losing everything if you don't cover yourself with clever bureaucracy and by using the correct terminology to describe your business practice. But it may be the closest we can get in the workforce to Oscar Wilde's idea that a person can only flourish when working artistically and independently of money and tyranny. 'It does not matter what he is,' he wrote, 'as long as he realises the perfection of the soul within him.'

Cottage industry is also the general direction in which things seem to be going anyway. Since 2008, a huge number of people have entered self-employment through necessity. The Royal Society of Arts suggest the ranks of the self-employed in Britain will soon outnumber the more drearily employed (five million people in 2015, due to overtake the employed in 2017), which is quite the victory for personal autonomy and the throwing wrenches into the big wheels of The Trap. Meanwhile, the government use those same figures to claim credit for increased employment, the dicks.

If you want to escape employment into self-employment, try to pave the way to that Shangri-La while still employed. Use your current job – or at least your downtime during your current job – to build a viable client base and to develop your skills. Try not to freak out and hand in your notice until you've proven to yourself that you can be successful in this mode. As anyone with an office job knows, most of your time at work is spent skiving or doing useless shit. There's even a word for when workers just sit around wasting company time: *presenteeism*. Use some of this time as a presentee to 'maximise your skill set', as a career-jockey might say. Even Houdini started as an attentive locksmith's apprentice. All of this will provide a safety net: you need to make yourself re-employable in case your escape plan fails.

## ESCAPE ROUTES FOR THE COMPLETELY OUTRAGEOUS ESCAPOLOGIST

**Live in the woods.** Why not live in the woods like Thoreau or a hermit? I'm slightly kidding (my tongue is always somewhat in my cheek) but I'm slightly serious too, because one really could do it. In 2014, *GQ* magazine reported on an American hermit: *'For nearly 30 years, a phantom haunted the woods of Central Maine. Unseen and unknown, he lived in secret, creeping into homes in the dead of night and* *surviving on what he could steal. To the spooked locals, he became a legend – or maybe a myth. They wondered how he could possibly be real. Until one day last year, the hermit came out of the forest.'* Doesn't that excite? That there might be people – 'phantoms' – on the fringes of society, in our collective peripheral vision, living differently to us? If full-blown, traditional hermitage does nothing for you, there are more established ways of setting up home in the woods.

Lin Yutang, discussing the philosophy of Tsesse writes, 'It is a poor philosophy that teaches us to escape from human society all together…The highest ideal of Chinese thought is a man who does not have to escape from human society and human life in order to preserve his original, happy nature. He is only a second-rate recluse, still slave to his environment, who has to escape the cities and live away in the mountains in solitude. The Great Recluse is the City Recluse because he has sufficient mastery over himself not to be afraid of his surroundings. He is therefore the great Monk (the *kaoseng*) who returns to human society to eat well and drink wine and mix with women, without detriment to his own soul…Those are the best cynics who are half-cynics.' I agree! And it feels good to have my personal lifestyle confirmed by a great intellectual. And yet…and yet. Is there not an appeal to that life in the mountains? At least today, one might have the mountain life and still return to society frequently, enjoying both flavours of Tsessean cynicism.

My friend and *New Escapologist* contributor Rob West and his family, for example, are building a beautiful home in the forests of British Columbia. Rob writes: 'We returned to Canada after a decade in London, UK, with a small child in tow and decided to set-up a sustainable twenty-first century homestead on 5.65 acres of fir, alder and meadow on Gabriola Island, British Columbia, Canada.' You can follow their exploits (with plenty of photographs charting the house's development and the beautiful wildlife around it) at thehandcraftedlife.com. Rob tells me he learned his skills from a group called The

Mud Girls Natural Building Collective, who are also worth looking up if you're thinking of an escape to the woods.

There's a fellow called Ben Law whom I originally learnt about on Channel 4's *Grand Designs* some years ago. On *Grand Designs* he built a woodland home using time-honoured natural building techniques and a very modest budget. There were strokes of pure genius in his design: the fact that he built his house using the proportions of standard British hay bales so he could slot them easily into the cavity wall as natural insulation once the structure was up struck me as genius. I also remember that he enlisted helpers willing to learn his construction techniques instead of being paid in money, which also struck me as highly Escapological in spirit, in that it uses knowledge in place of dough. Escapologists need money too, but even in a finance-oriented escape plan like Jacob's Early Retirement Extreme, expertise is the real key and money a tool. Ben Law still lives in the house he built on *Grand Designs* and runs a cottage industry (if you'll overlook the rubbish pun of that) writing books and running courses about his particular brand of woodland house building.

There was Mark Boyle who lived in a caravan, powered his laptop and telephone with solar power, ate home-grown and foraged food, and spent his time writing for activism. None of this cost a penny after the initial setup. He had a *Guardian* column for a while called 'Moneyless Man' and there would often be pictures of him looking all sexy with his shirt off or looking completely mental with wild apples balanced in the brim of his wacky sunhat. According to his new website he's now in the process of setting up a 'fully localised, land-based gift economy' in Ireland. I always liked the way of living he promoted in the *Guardian* column: it's not quite hermitage but it doesn't require the kind of skills and vision of building a house as Rob West is doing. One could theoretically act on the impulse to live as Mark Boyle lived almost immediately and with no special training. It'd be easier to learn as you went along than having to learn to build a whole house.

Another *New Escapologist* contributor, Nicolette Stewart, lives in a 'tiny home'. This is part of a recent post-2008 movement: the trading of big homes for small but beautiful wooden homes, sometimes built from scratch or from a kit, though Nic says: 'It feels a bit absurd to call it a movement. When I think of the people from the pages of the history books forced upon us in school, I see seven-person families in one-room cabins, sixteen people crammed into small tenement rooms in New York City, tepees, longhouses, and yurts – all of them tiny dwellings. Today, folks who say they live in tiny houses are usually talking about structures under 500 square feet, though forms vary drastically.'

Tiny homes sometimes resemble sheds, shacks, caravans or specially designed miniature mansions. They come with many advantages. Nic says: 'Being able to live within one's means is important for the Escapologist interested in unfinanced schemes and pleasures. A house that you can obtain or build and maintain cheaply solves the shelter problem without the required years of toil ... Living in a tiny home has been a key element in my own escape from the grind, though I came to the lifestyle through a desire for a like-minded community rather than a desire to live in a small space. But when you have less space, it becomes impractical to collect too many possessions, a habit which will help you stay out of the office. My home, a six metre wooden caravan known as a *Bauwagen*, is cheap and simple to maintain, mobile and was given to me for free. These thing have only added to its charm and usefulness as a tool of escape.'

And then there's Gee Vaucher and Penny Rimbaud, formerly of the punk rock band Crass, who stuck to their anti-capitalist principles after their years in the band and set up an open house in Epping Forest in Essex. It's called Dial House and it's often described as a paradise. It does indeed look beautiful. A *Guardian* journalist called Emily Mackay in 2014 described it as 'an incredible place. Every surface sparkles with care and love and craft: a very English anarchist idyll, heaving with carvings, mosaics, stained glass, fascinating bookshelves and, in one corner, a tiny dancing Shiva proudly sporting a sticker emblazoned with the words UP YOUR ARSE.' Vaucher and Rimbaud bought the property at auction in the nineties after renting it cheaply since 1967. 'The idea was to create a safe house for people,' Vaucher told Mackay, 'People know that if they have nothing, they can at least come here for a night and get their strength back and be fed and watered and hopefully go off with a better heart.'

Thoreau wrote from his tiny, self-built house at Walden Pond, 'I went to the woods because I wished to live deliberately, to front only the essential facts of life, and see if I could not learn what it had to teach, and not, when I came to die, discover that I had not lived.'

'Am I an outsider? I don't really know,' said Gee Vaucher, 'I don't care, really. If they wanna call me an outsider, that's fine, they wanna call me something else, it's fine. I just get on with my work.'

**Profiting on waste.** My Montreal friend Martin is a garbage picker. He makes a living by selling things he finds in the garbage. Like me, Martin wasn't fond of going to work so he quit. Where some people in a similar situation might have been moved to pore over the classified ads in search of another less shit job, Martin quietly took to walking around Montreal like a *flâneur*. Doing so, he noticed the huge number of bin bags put out on trash collection days. He was already of a non-consumerist mindset but was still surprised by the volume of waste being produced. This happens partly because we have a culture in which most commodities are considered disposable and partly because people with jobs don't have the time or energy to dispose of things productively by gifting, recycling or selling them. It's easier to bin a thing or dump it on the kerbside.

Martin took note of the things people were ditching. This can't have been difficult: the city streets are strewn with abandoned furniture, appliances, computers, bags of clothing. Often, these things have not yet reached the natural end of their lives, are still functioning and usable, and sometimes have not been used at all. Moved by this wastefulness, he began salvaging what he could and set up a blog (www. garbagefinds.com) encouraging other people to salvage from the streets. The idea is to intercept prematurely junked items before they're condemned to landfill. Martin found he could make money, even a living, from kerb finds. This is not a new idea: rag-and-bone men used to do a similar thing in Britain up until the 1970s. After salvaging what he can from the streets, Martin lists it on eBay, Craigslist and Etsy, holds increasingly famous yard sales, and arranges transactions via his website.

The blog, incidentally, is good fun. For the armchair garbage explorer, it's fascinating. He routinely finds 1960s print ephemera, antiques, canned goods, crates of untouched beer. My favourite post so far must be the one about 'the largest pile of garbage I've ever seen', the result of a house clearance after someone's death. It seemed as if an entire lifetime's accumulation had been dumped unceremoniously on the pavement. This pile must have stretched for an entire city block. It makes you think about material legacy: what will happen to *my* stuff when I'm dead? Will my treasured possessions end up hastily dumped on a kerbside by a landlord or relative who just doesn't give a shit? It's another good reason not to own so much stuff.

As to the specifics of how to profit from other people's waste, the main thing is to get out there and start looking. You could do it right now if you were so motivated. Even so, Martin offers tips. Patrol on foot or by bicycle, he says, especially on trash collection days when waste is most ripe for interception. Learn to recognise a likely pile of trash and to learn to recognise evidence of the dreaded bedbug in soft furnishings. You can find an item's value, he says, by searching through eBay's completed listings.

Poking through rubbish is not everyone's idea of a good time. It's worse than work, you might think: sifting through other people's trash is probably the very situation most people are trying to avoid by staying employed. But Martin has come to it of his own volition through a sense of environmental and civic duty: much as I suggested earlier, as people would in a world with Citizen's Income. He occupies a niche by redistributing discarded goods, capitalising on a sorrowful waste. It's not for everyone (I for one admire but don't emulate him) but it shows that ways of making money and occupying time usefully outside employment are real, and that your living can be in tune with your personal values. It also shows that, if you're willing to get your hands dirty, you'll never be destitute or have to get up at 7am to report to a job you hate.

**Do what you like.** Michael Palin, in an interview with the *Idler* said that the best way to avoid work is to do what you like to do. The idea is that an activity can hardly be called work if you're making money doing your favourite combination of things. Indeed, that's what Palin did: his three careers have been comedy, acting, and travel. His sympathies are mirrored in a hard-to-find 1949 book called *How to Avoid Work*. The author of this book, one William J. Reilly – for whom I like to fancy we get the expression 'life of Reilly' – encourages you to retreat into yourself, work out precisely what it is you like to do, and find a way of getting paid for it. It seems like a bit of a rip-off when you buy a book called *How to Avoid Work* which still insists in sending you off to a workplace, but you can't fault the logic that work is only work when you feel like a slave more than a freeman.

The best way to do this, I believe, is to take a mini-retirement. If you can wangle a few months away from your job (you might especially deserve it if you happen to be clinically depressed or anxious as a result of work) or if you have enough savings to quit your job with the intention of having six months or a year of free time before looking for a new one, you'll create an oasis of free time in which to regroup. Even if you're not thinking of leaving the rat race permanently, a mini-retirement is no bad thing. Instead of waiting until you're 65 to take it all at the end, take your retirement in instalments throughout your career and you'll probably be a lot happier.

But I mention mini-retirements here as a potential regrouping strategy: take the time away from work (and ideally away from other nuisance commitments too) in order to figure out precisely what you'd like to do. What are your favourite tools to work with? What kind of skills do you most like to exercise? How do you most want to be seen by the world? Would you like to help people or do you prefer to be alone? What, more than anything else in the world, would you like to recreate yourself as, if money weren't an issue? Can you come up with a practical plan for getting to this new job? Don't force yourself into asking these questions right away: enjoy some time off and the answers will probably come to you after some weeks of unhassled, unhurried leisure.

A word of caution should be voiced when trying to discover what it is you'd most like to do: you may like cakes, but do you really want to be a baker? Something may seem like a calling but the attendant duties of the job may not be what you were looking for. Consider the true nature of the project you're looking for as well as the end result of it. A common but perfectly wise piece of advice is to hook up with someone who actually does what you're thinking of doing. If you want to be a baker, track down a friendly-seeming baker (perhaps on Twitter or a web forum for bakers or by asking around in the pub) and invite them out for a coffee. It might be a good way of gauging the realities of a particular job or caper (besides, actually talking to people with experience different to your own is an interesting and fun thing to do anyway).

**Understand that a penny saved is a penny earned.** The reason so many people think they need to work full-time is because of the staggering number of obligations they have: television licences or satellite television packages need to be paid for, as do cars; home entertainment; restaurant meals; concert or sports tickets; cigarettes; digital toys; resort vacations. Severing your need for these things, realising that they're follies, will mean you don't have to work full-time at all. Turn your back on them one by one and replace them with free or low-cost pursuits. It may sound miserly or in conflict with the good life but only if you're still believing the lie told to all worker–consumers that expensive things are good things. It isn't true. The best and most interesting theatre, for example, is usually cheap or free and happens in arts festivals and universities and in fringe theatre: the worst theatre in the world takes place on Broadway in New York and in London's West End where tickets are very expensive. The entirety of the world's literature is available for free in the library. Sex, the driving force behind all human culture, is free. A healthy lifestyle of exercise and good nutrition is free. Even millionaires have to drink water, the main source of which is practically free. When you have half the desire of the average person you become twice as rich. If we want to make enough money to escape with a reasonable standard of comfort, we need to reconsider the values typically instilled into the worker–consumer. The idea that wealth is success; that worthy partners are drawn to your money; that a car is the only way to travel; that a career will be fulfilling; that home ownership is in any way better than renting; that you need the expensive shoes if you want to go for a run: we know that none of this is true. It's all been planted in your brain by advertising, by your own natural fear of failure, by status anxiety and the strongest force in the universe: peer pressure. Silence these false ideas! Ignore them. Slow down. Work less. Escape is closer than you think.

## WRINGHAM'S ESCAPE PLAN

We need not commit to just one of the above escape plans. One could take elements of each and mash them up into a unique, personal escape plan taking one's own temperaments, skills and resources into account. What follows is an escape plan originally published in the third issue of *New Escapologist*, fine-tuned for the sophisticated modern day hominid. It looks simple but deceptively so, informed by rational and mainstream business techniques like downsizing, liquidation and geo-arbitrage. It's also not really a plan, more a report of precisely what I did when I escaped my first bullshit job at the astonishingly impudent age of 26. When employed, it is nigh on impossible to find the time and energy to formulate an escape plan. This lack of time and energy when employed is probably why most people don't recognise that escape is even an option. The aim of this escape plan is to buy yourself the time and energy with which to develop a long-term solution.

My plan assumes you want to flee a life of white-collar servitude. It is from here that you might begin:

1. Save money. You'll need moderately healthy financial reserves to fund the first weeks or months of your escape. Aim to save a useful sum of money. I recommend £10,000, though the more you save, the more comfortable you can be for a while. This sum is your escape fund. This will be harder to achieve if you're in debt or subscribe to unnecessary services. In order to reach your target more quickly, sell unnecessary assets. Convert unwieldy possessions into mobile, liquid cash. You might only want to do this for high value goods: selling individual DVDs is time-consuming and seldom lucrative, but that's up to you. It's good to be rid of them anyway, in order to maximise mobility.

2. Use your job as a career gym. Like the convict who uses the prison gym to get in shape, get as much experience as you can and as many flavours as possible: do favours for people, run meetings, attend training courses, generate ideas, talk to the boss, talk to the cleaners, manage a budget, write reports, deliver presentations, make the tea. Record all of this on your CV. Use your time at work to maximise your skillset. This will provide a safety net:

you need to make yourself re-employable in case your escape plan fails.

3. Cull your expenses. It's probably obvious that your income must be greater than your outgoings. Bills can be avoided if you gradually eliminate your dependencies on the services for which you pay. Get rid of your car and become a pedestrian. Get rid of your mobile phone by telling people to use your house phone or email instead. Get rid of any other false liberty that only results in bills. You will soon find an optimum outgoing: the true cost of living. It will be much less than it was before your elimination process and will usually be the sum of your rent, food, house phone, council or municipal tax and electricity. Let us call this sum Cost of Living, for it will come into play again later.

4. Quit your job. It can be tempting to send your boss a letter along the lines of 'Dear Boss, I quit. Kiss my bottom and eat my dust. Good day!' or to hire a barbershop quartet to deliver the message in song, as apparently someone in America recently did. By all means do those things if you like (and tell me about it by email and I'll feature you in *New Escapologist*) but I'd more sagely advise telling your boss in person, assuring her that you're willing to work your contractual notice period, and presenting her with a short, unemotional, gracious but unambiguous letter. There are templates available for such letters online. This is the end of your career. Have a nice, dark beer to celebrate.

5. Give your house or apartment keys back to the landlord. Put your stuff into storage (I can vouch for a company called Safestore, but there are lots of others). Cancel all direct debits, except for the one paying for your storage. Up until now, everything has been prologue. This is the real beginning of your escape.

6. Take your escape fund and fly to somewhere vibrant and cheap. I can vouch for Berlin and Montreal, but there are many places in the world that would qualify. Rent a cheap apartment there. Immigrant-heavy areas (such as Kreutzberg in Berlin and Saint-Henri in Montreal) are culturally alive and financially inexpensive. They have good food, public transport and are popular with intelligent, hip, bohemian types. Use up to half of your escape fund to enjoy a long and restful vacation. Explore the city; relax cheaply or for free in parks, museums or libraries; make friends; invite old friends to visit; eat, drink and read. Enjoy yourself and vigorously celebrate your escape.

7. Invent a cottage industry. Use the rest of your mini-retirement – however much time your escape fund allows – to invent a way to ensure you'll never have to go back to work. Remind yourself why you wanted to escape in the first place: the drudgery, the early mornings, the mindless submission, the waiting on pay cheques. Never forget the conditions from which you're fleeing. Think up a cottage industry for yourself. It must be either (a) fully automated, requiring little work on your behalf or (b) fun and in tune with your values and interests. In either event, the income generated by your cottage industry must be at least equal to your Cost of Living. Don't try too hard. Through your period of inactivity, you'll probably discover over a poolside Margarita what you want to do. As explained above, this could be a cottage industry, an automated company or an investment plan like Jacob Lund Fisker's. You might even want to consider diversifying your plan by using a combination of these models.

8. Set your plan in motion from your apartment or from a cosy space in a public library. When the money starts to come in, you will have found yourself a vocation. You have escaped. You can now

begin your new life, wherever and in whatever circumstances you want to begin it: tiny home in Germany, apartment in London, hand-built house in the woods, anything you like.

Try it. The worst-case scenario is that your cottage industry fails and you have to go back to office drudgery, tail between your legs. If this happens, you will at least have enjoyed an extended vacation, lived abroad, tried and failed at entrepreneurship. This is better than what you'd have been doing otherwise. You'll have some interesting items to put on your CV and some great stories to tell in the pub. Best of all, there's nothing to stop you from trying the whole thing again.

## GOODBYE TO ALL THAT!

It is possible to escape the world of work. We might do it wisely and robustly as Jacob Lund Fisker did. We might passionately throw it all in and find dignity in a not-traditionally-glamorous area as Martin the garbage picker did. We might start a flourishing business. We might start your own *automated* business like Tim Ferris did and watch the money roll in. We might 'do what you like' as Michael Palin did. One might become the stay-at-home partner in a two-person domestic team or, if one doesn't want that as a sole occupation, we could be a home-based artistic partner as Joseph Heath suggests. Where such strategies are too rich for our blood, there are the lower-income but perfectly conventional working modes like part-time and temporary work so long as we make the most of the advantages they offer.

The solutions are there if we want them. It may not always be easy or palatable at first to set up a business or to decrease our spending to make part-time work feasible, but it beats the hell out of reporting for duty eight hours per day, five days per week *for 40 years*.

To think of it another way, it ostensibly takes 11 to 17 years of formal education to get a moderately well paid but soul-destroying desk job of dubious value to society. It may well take the same again to build the perfect business, but hopefully it won't take that long and we might find that it only takes a year. And, of course, we don't need the *perfect* business: just one that's good enough to let us escape.

These are the ways we can escape the world of work. They can be acted upon individually. They do not require massive support systems, professional assistance, huge expenditure, bank loans, political activism, or a change in the social or political consciousness. They may not be wholly glamorous or instantly appealing but are they worse than the alternative? They are not dependent upon the unlikely good fortune of a lottery jackpot, an *X Factor* win, or finding a magic lantern in an Oxfam shop. If we take our time and commit to a well reasoned plan, it's possible to escape the conventional workplace once and for all. Shackle broken. Goodbye to all that.

# ESCAPE CONSUMPTION

*The apparatus is inexpensive, consisting of a little
silk paper and a couple of blonde hairs.*
— Houdini

## GET OUT OF DEBT

Consumerism is the main reason we end up working so much. If we worked to provide ourselves with the basics – food, shelter, clothes, the odd treat – money wouldn't be a problem. We'd either work a two-day week or simply retire with a bulging purse at the age of 33. As it stands, the consumer economy has made us insatiable. Thanks to consumerism, we're always hungry for more. And if we're always hungry for more, we can't possibly join the good life. Get this: you're under no obligation to remain a victim of consumerism through addiction to its conveniences.

The appetite for consumer goods is so great that most of us are in debt. The average household in Britain owes something like £3,200 on credit cards, overdrafts and loans. This doesn't include the average household mortgage, which is something like £75,000 but for some reason isn't seen as a big deal. There's also the horde of unethical companies offering payday loans to poor people via adverts on crap TV channels that, though a tempting solution to short-term problems, will result in huge repayments potentially for a very long time.

Debt is unfreedom. If you owe 75 grand, your net worth is *minus* 75 grand. Every day you work under such a debt, you're not making money but paying back a debt. 'Anyone work for the bank?' comedian Simon Munnery asks his audience to a confused silence. 'Anyone in debt?' results in an ironic cheer. 'Who d'you think you work for then?' Debt is the worst thing in the world. If you're not in debt, you have the power to walk silently away from your day job. If you're in debt, you do not have that power: you'll be trapped until, one way or another, you repay the debt. If you're working to pay off a debt, you are a slave.

The best way to avoid debt is to not get into it. Don't buy a house for £200,000 if you don't have £200,000 to buy it. Don't go shopping with a credit card if your bank balance is less than you plan to spend that day. Pay as you go, in other words, and don't get tied into anything. But for many of us, it's too late. We're all prone to slip-ups. When student grants were completely phased out in Britain in the greedy 1980s, they were replaced with student loans. That's worse than replacing them with nothing! If they'd replaced grants with nothing at all, only those who could afford it would have gone to university: hardly an ideal situation but the new student loans system means people going to university who can't afford it and entering into 20 years – perhaps a lifetime – of debt. Of course, that's perfect for the neo-liberal agenda and the consumer economy: a population of young debtors is a great opportunity. It's surprising that they've not tried to cripple us even earlier in life by offering competitive rate 'birthday loans' to newborn babies via well-meaning expecting parents. I'm certain that someone out there will have had that idea and is currently awaiting the legal go-ahead.

If you're currently in debt, you're further behind an Escapologist who is simply poor or worth zero pounds. You first project must be to pay off the debt before you can have a chance at freedom. Financial Blogger Mr Money Mustache advises seeing debt as an emergency situation: 'it's like being surrounded by a swarm of killer bees,' he says, 'covering every square inch of your body. Or alternatively, you could think of it as being in a cauldron full of boiling lava and poisonous snakes.' This is not just a diagnosis – an accurate description of debt as a pressing situation – but a course of action. If you really were covered in killer bees, you'd act quickly and impulsively, perhaps rolling on the ground in an attempt to squash the bees or get them off you no matter what. You must treat debt the same way: *getitoffgetitoffgetitoff!!!*

You're going to have to act quickly. A debt is like a fire in that it can spread rapidly: the interest on each debt will accumulate and you'll end up paying more than you borrowed. With this in mind, pay your most expensive debts first. For all my complaining about student loans (though I still maintain that they're evil) they're actually quite cheap: 16% APR credit card debts or 20% Wonga debts should be destroyed first, as they're the most dangerous. Granted, you're unlikely to be able to do this with a mortgage. My solution, if it's not too glib, is to not take out a mortgage in the first place. If you have one already, you might even consider reversing the process by selling your house: imagine the feeling of release when you drop that millstone. Renting is great: you don't have to worry about repairs, factor or condo fees, property tax or the burden of ownership. Renters are far more mobile too, mobility, the chief concern of Escapologists. The commonest objection to renting is that renters 'pour their money down a hole' but thanks to the interest accrued on a mortgage and the possibility that you'll actually never pay off the whole thing, it's true of home-owners too. It's just a matter of who you prefer to throw money to: a landlord or a bank. I like to take my chances with a landlord, because they're usually individual people (who might even be rather nice!) rather than terrifying international bureaucracies. The renting versus ownership debate has gone on for decades (centuries?), but as property prices spiral ever upwards and jobs become poorer and poorer paid, any claim to ownership's superiority is increasingly moot. The debate also eclipses the fact that there are other ways to find shelter beyond renting and owning: consider some of the modes – tiny homes, caravans, tents, squats, intentional communities – already mentioned and I know that there are others.

Always pay more than the minimum. The terms of a debt might demand you pay back 30 per cent of it per month or something, but you can usually surprise the moneylenders by paying off 50 per cent, 80 per cent, or ideally, 100 per cent if you can. Go all out to destroy a debt. Stamp it out.

Save money elsewhere – everywhere! – and prioritise debt repayment. Again, it's an emergency. You shouldn't be buying expensive groceries or gym subscriptions or cigarettes if you have debts to pay. Debts may not be fun things to throw money at but they must be your priority. Track what you actually spend in order to find new areas of economy: a pound saved on a grocery bill is a pound paid off your debt.

Work extra hard. You won't see that advice very often in this book, which is hopefully how you can tell I'm serious. Work extra hours, extra shifts, extra jobs. Work in this rare, unique case is freedom. Buy back your freedom. Use all of your might to clamber back up to the surface.

If things are really bad and you can't see a fast way out of the swarm of killer bees, speak with a debt counsellor at the Citizens Advice Bureau. They can help you to negotiate with the moneylenders, set up payment plans, and occasionally reduce it to a far smaller monthly payment.

Finally, learn from *The Hitch-hiker's Guide to the Galaxy*, and don't panic. Oh, and never, *ever*, take a loan to pay a loan. Once you're free, cut up your credit cards and develop a life in which you don't need one. Pay as you go. Have a cigar. Rejoice and be free. But only once you're back on top.

## THE NATURE OF RELATIVE WEALTH

It has been observed by the sarcastic that while money can't buy you love, it can buy you a lot of fun. Well, yes. And without money for the basics of life, we'd be in trouble. If unhappiness is malnutrition and discomfort, it could be argued that money *can* buy happiness inasmuch as it can fend off malnutrition and discomfort.

But how much is enough? How much money and stuff is required to make us happy? Is it enough to be nutritionally sated and physically comfortable or do we require a little more? If so, how much more? At what point does desire become greed? Quite a few people have attempted to answer this question. Aristotle developed his 'golden mean'. Economist John Maynard Keynes had a figure in mind when he predicted a society wealthy enough to be free from toil by 2030 if we chose to do so. Journalist John Naish perhaps has the right idea by suggesting that as long as we have what we need plus a little more than the neighbours, we've hit the jackpot.

Naish's point about having a little more than the neighbours is a good one. Not only does it sagely hint that moving to a cheaper, less middle-class neighbourhood might let you win the battle without struggling to earn so much (because if your neighbours don't buzz around in sports cars, you won't be tempted to compete with very much) but also that our feelings of 'wealth' or 'enoughness' are *relative*. Even millionaires must feel insecure if all they see around them are billionaires.

And so we get to 'competitive consumption': the idea that we have to go one better than the Joneses. Joseph Heath describes this as 'a race to the bottom'. If you see that your neighbour has a good car and feel moved to respond by getting a *great* car, she'll retaliate sooner or later by getting another great car or an *excellent* car. It's a competition to see who is the best at consumption, but there can be no winners because you both end up with more car than you need and working hard to pay for them. It's like a Laurel and Hardy routine.

Competitive consumption is a law of diminishing returns. After a certain point – a point reached more quickly than we may think – material wealth does not contribute to happiness. This might not be a problem (lots of things don't contribute to happiness – jiffy bags, toadstools, advertising – it may not be their purpose) if it weren't for the fact that they result in negative externalities: inelegance, hoarding, the wanton expenditure of natural resources, air pollution, wage slavery.

In other words, consumption beyond meeting the basics and a little more for luxury, is not worth the potentially considerable sacrifices. One of these sacrifices is the good life. This was observed by the economists Edward and Robert Skidelsky in their amazing book *How Much is Enough?* They identify insatiability as one of the great problems of our age and end the book by recommending we find a way to curb insatiability. Capitalism, in their view, was a Mephistophelian pact: we needed to shake hands with the Devil in order to provide food for the masses, to get organised, to cater for our wants, to minimise the back-breaking labour, to make space for the arts. But on the sinister flip side, the capitalist machine offers us so much more: iPhones, plastic toys, Hollywood movies based on board games, disposable paper tissues, disposable baby nappies, clothes designed to survive just five washes before falling apart, clothes designed to go out of fashion, appliances designed to explode after a year and be deliberately succeeded by an apparently superior model. There are whole industries producing little but inessential waste. Mountains of expired washing machines and a pit of remaindered Atari games in the New Mexico desert were not part of the deal: these things happened because of insatiability. Insatiability was an unforeseen fault in the system and it is proving very difficult to debug.

## THE NATURE OF COMPETITIVE CONSUMPTION

In their excellent book, *The Rebel Sell*, Joseph Heath and Andrew Potter tell us that rebel gestures (tattoos, piercings, street parties, pilgrimages to Burning Man, purple hair) may be festive but don't actually change anything: they're just products in the same way that seemingly mainstream non-rebel trends are products. In fact, they say, the entire counterculture's message that mainstream culture serves to repress us and to hone a kind of conformist society in which everyone aspires to live in the same suburban kit houses with the same kinds of cars and the same haircuts, is a fallacy. The counterculture seems to think that, unless you're a rebel, you're a Sim. This, point out Heath and Potter, has not been the case since the 1950s and that mainstream society today – the consumer economy – is entirely based around *distinction*. Nobody wants to see themselves as conformists, nor do they. When the starchy salaryman sees his neighbour's impressive new car and decides to go one better, he does not do this to conform, but to distinguish himself. Those rebel gestures like piercings and whatnot are just another embodiment of this: they were not even 'co-opted' by consumption; they were never anything other than another positional good. Rolex watch or pierced face, the motivation comes from the same place: the search for distinction, not conformity.

The deeper you get into thinking about positional goods and competitive consumption, the more interesting it gets. Much competitive consumption, write Heath and Potter, is 'defensive'. To illustrate, they provide two examples. In the first, a wealthy family member breaks the agreed-upon Christmas present budget and buys everyone first-rate gifts. The rest of the family are forced to act defensively: to buy more expensive or more luxurious gifts next year to avoid looking like thoughtless cheapskates. This is an act of defensive consumption: they may not want to spend money on top-notch Christmas presents, but they have been socially shamed into doing so by the profligate relative last year. In Heath and Potter's second example, people start buying big cars – SUVs – and whenever there's a car crash, they survive while people in dinky little smart cars do not. This leads to a driver essentially being forced into buying an SUV as a form of defence: she may not want a gas-guzzling, air-polluting 'gated community on wheels', but if she doesn't want to die in a collision, she'll feel moved to drive a big car.

Competitive consumption then, is not always about showing off and distinguishing oneself, but is in fact 'defensive', it can be extremely difficult for us to willingly opt out of consumption. We risk (as in the Christmas presents example) social ostracism or (as in the cars example) actual harm. But there is a way out of this Chinese Finger Trap, or rather a way to avoid falling into it. It's called minimalism.

## MINIMALISM

'It is the privilege of the gods to want nothing, and of godlike men to want little, ' said Diogenes of Sinope, not the most popular man in all of Sinope since he lived in a sort of dustbin in the middle of the market-place, had a penchant for wanking in public and shitting in the theatre. But he *was* wise. Minimalism, one of the life tenets he advocated, is a way of removing the non-essential things from life so that we might focus on the important ones: the objects and activities that give our lives meaning, pleasure, and value.

Few things offered by consumption are essential and are therefore dispensable. So why not dispense with them and get on with living? This is how minimalism offers a solution, perhaps the best solution, to the problem of consumption: in prompting us to ask what's essential it exposes almost everything else offered by consumption to scrutiny. It doesn't exactly break the collective action problem but it provides a valid alternative to getting involved with it at all. There has, ironically, been an awful lot said about minimalism in books and on websites. But to live minimally really just requires adherence to two simple objectives. Here's *The Condensed Minimalist*:

1. Don't buy or otherwise acquire anything you can't eat
2. Rid yourself of anything not frequently useful or
   aesthetically pleasing to you

When it comes to the intersection of possessions and living well, that is the whole of the law. Minimalism need not be a difficult lifestyle to adopt but its benefits cannot be understated. It can even be fun as you find intriguing new ways to live as a minimalist. It allows you to gain control of your surroundings, to improve mental clarity and presence of mind and to maximise mobility and autonomy. It is primarily offered here, however, as a way to escape consumption in order to escape work and to enjoy the good life. When you don't need (or even want) much stuff, you don't need much money to pay for it. And if you don't need much money, you can afford to work less. If you don't need much money, you're extremely unlikely to go into debt. It's a very simple equation: less stuff = more freedom.

If some of the escape routes from work described in Chapter 9 seem financially impractical for your circumstances, minimalism will serve as a companion solution. If, for example, the reduced income of part-time work will not support your lifestyle, it's entirely possible that your life-style is unnecessarily expensive. Less stuff might enable you to move to a smaller house, resulting in a smaller financial commitment. Minimal-ism is the most important discipline to embrace if you want to turn your back on both consumption and work. If you commit to only one activity or philosophy promoted by this book, let it be minimalism. 'If you want a golden rule that will fit everything, this is it,' said William Morris, 'have nothing in your home that you do not know to be useful or believe to be beautiful.'

A spatula is useful for making stir-fries or flipping burger patties. A piece of art might be beautiful. Perhaps that same piece of art is also useful in some way, perhaps for impressing guests, and maybe a spatula could be seen as beautiful in the right light. By William Morris's criteria, both are welcome – perhaps doubly welcome – in a home. Less welcome would be multiple spatulas (because only one can be useful) and so many paintings as to detract from their individual beauty or the beauty of the home in general. Also unwelcome: too many trinkets or *tchotchkes*, too many toys, old or irrelevant administrative papers, loose-leaf binders filled with high school reports or even high school work, packaging from appliances, shoes that don't fit properly, clothes you don't love, unused sports equipment or kitchen gadgets.

Stripping away the things that don't matter (and refusing to acquire more of which does not matter) allows us to focus better on the things that remain. The things that remain, you'll discover, bear a striking resemblance to (or help to facilitate) the tenets of the good life. If the potential to free you from the shackles of consumption and debt doesn't convince you that minimalism is the way forward, you might want to consider some of the other benefits of a minimalist lifestyle:

It enables **mobility**. Few people consider freedom unimportant and to an Escapologist it's the primary goal. We value liberty and the right to live with few restrictions, yet we typically dedicate our lives to acquiring a permanent residence and a substantial cache of possessions ('a bunch of stuff with a cover on it' is George Carlin's description of a house). Instead of spending money on travel, we allow it to be swallowed up by a mortgage. By losing some materialist weight and tempering our desire for goods we can use our financial and intellectual resources more wisely and follow the mobile ideal.

Minimalism is **good for the environment**. If everyone adopted a minimalist lifestyle and there was no more demand for non-essential consumer goods, fewer materials would need extracting from the Earth to make them. Reduction is the least observed of the three *R*'s of environmentalism ('reduce, reuse, recycle') but it's probably the most important. Reuse and recycling are sensible measures in an over-productive society, but why not neutralise the problem of overproduc-tion at the source? Instead of choosing to act efficiently at the end of a product's life cycle by reusing or recycling it, we should stop said product from being made in the first place by eliminating consumer demand for it. If the rainforests must be burned and the oceans poisoned to cater for the essentials of human life, then so be it and we'll call it an inevitable pity; but for that to happen in the name of games consoles, cell phones and chocolate fountains is a wanton and avoidable shame.

Minimalism enables **intellectual focus**. Fewer possessions mean fewer things with which to concern ourselves and less information to routinely process. When we make our homes into minimalist sanctuaries, we're able to regain focus and to enjoy greater presence of mind.

Minimalists enjoy greater **autonomy**. Every object you own has a financial cost attached to it. As well as the first cost of acquiring it, an item must be stored, maintained, sometimes transported and ultimately disposed of. There's a cost attached to each of these moments of ownership. The more we own, the more expensive our lifestyles become and the more money we need to sustain it. Having fewer possessions reduces our need to work so hard. If we jettison half of our possessions and start working part-time, we can use the extra time to follow intellectual, spiritual or physical pursuits.

Minimalism allows for a **heightened appreciation of objects**. Suppose you lead a life of extreme minimalism and reside in a white box. When you choose to bring an object into this space, it has a greater significance or relevance than the same object acquired by a hoarder. Instead of being another thing in a cluttered space, an object owned by a minimalist has significance and quiddity. You can savour the beauty and benefit from the utility of this significant item as Epicurus would have done.

Minimalism can **go beyond physical concerns**. Consider the meetings or traditions or relationships or regimens in life, which we don't need and could be expunged from future editions of your diary altogether. Consider the digital entities that weigh upon our consciousnesses: the number of newsfeeds, the number of people you follow on Twitter, the number of non-friends you have on Facebook, the mailing lists to which you're inadvertently subscribed. Can any of it be expunged? The less information and noise competing for your attention, the happier and less stressed out you will be. The fewer time commitments you have, the more time you'll have for the things that matter: family, friends, the good life.

Minimalism is a personal **protest against the culture of more**, a meaningful protest capable of changing our lives without necessarily trying to change the culture or the political climate. By adopting a minimalist lifestyle, you serve as an example of someone who rejects the culture of more.

As a point of lurid interest, refusing to buy anything may be anti-materialist but it is sadly not anti-capitalist even if that's your intention. When you stop buying things but continue to earn money through work, your earnings continue to serve the capitalist machine. The bank in which you store your wealth 'spends' your savings when they invest it. (That's why the bank pays you interest: as a reward for letting them play with your money.) Perversely, saving and spending actually amount to the same thing so far as the economy is concerned. But when you reduce your income as well as your spending, it actually *does* hurt the capitalist machine! If your motivation to engage in minimalism is to smash the system, you must remember to reduce your income as well as your spending. Thus, only Escapological minimalism, since it aims to reduce work as well as consumption, will genuinely throw a spanner in the works of capitalism. Quitting your job could be one of the most radical things you ever do.

## PRACTICALITIES OF MINIMALISM

I can't get enough minimalism. In life, I'm down to brass tacks. The only way I could be further minimalist is body *bonsai*, but that's where I draw the line. I don't want to end up as a disembodied head in a jar asking, 'is this spinal cord strictly necessary?'

But that's just me. Everyone's idea of minimalism will be different. Our aesthetic tastes and utility needs are all different: I don't require a television set, preferring to read books or to stream videos on my laptop. Another person will like to have the television perpetually switched on, to channel hop, to watch talk shows and news and weather. To some, a telly provides value and pleasure and that's hunky-dory.

Anyway, here's some – hopefully universal – advice about minimalism. I developed it with my friend Tim, who is also a devout minimalist.

**Minimalism is not the same thing as decluttering**. A decluttering session is like a crash diet; it may have desirable short-term effects, but the old habits remain, the acquisition process continues, and so the core problem never goes away. A minimalist lifestyle is less about decluttering and more about developing some habits of mind:

It is important first to **learn of the disease**. Be aware that stuff accumulates of its own accord. No effort is required on your part for your drawers, shelves and cupboards to fill with junk. It happens almost as if by magic, but of course results from a lack of acquisitional restraint. Recognising this tendency, and the vigilance required to counterbalance it, is the first step towards a minimalist lifestyle.

Making **a habit of mini-clear outs** is probably the best way of keeping a minimalist lifestyle. Minimalism should be a gradual pruning process as in *bonsai*, or a neat and habitual process of cultivation as in tending a garden. It is not accomplished by launching a disruptive one-off campaign. The moment you take that last black bag to Oxfam, things will start to pile up again. Stop it getting out of hand by doing a single drawer or cupboard when the fancy takes you. If you catch yourself in an unsentimental mood one evening, throw out some burdensome objects you've been hanging onto. If you have not been able to rid yourself of something the first time round, you may be able to do so on a fourth or fifth attempt, as your sentimentality for an item diminishes.

**Stay organised**. The better organised you are, the less stuff you'll need. For example, if you don't lose your can-opener then you won't need a spare. Similarly, the less stuff you have, the easier it will be to keep yourself organised. The traditional maxim 'a place for everything and everything in its place' is easier to heed when you have fewer things: it's impossible to forget where your lawnmower lives if you don't own a lawnmower or, for that matter, a lawn. It is good to habitually consider ways of streamlining your life, of stripping out things you do not want or need. These should not be unattainable major upheavals but small, incremental improvements. An example of a small streamlining project is to organise your administrative papers: condemning old, succeeded, or no-longer relevant paperwork to the shredder is highly satisfying. After all, paperwork is not something you want in your life. For every inch won back from paperwork, an inch will open up for something better like books or, better still, clear empty space.

**Be bold**. With the exception of those things with true and deep sentimental value – the only photograph of a lost friend, the teddy bear with whom you spent a childhood – it's unusual to regret throwing something out. I usually forget about the discarded thingummy almost immediately. Keep the truly precious but know that anything else is expendable.

**Buy one, bin one** is a good policy. It's the 'dead men's shoes' of stuff management. Fancy a new shirt? Good idea. When you put it in your wardrobe, find your least favourite existing shirt and bin it. Better still, bin two. In this way the average quality of the things you own will go up and your clutter burden will go down.

For better or worse, gift giving is part of the fabric of human life. Presents are laced with social obligation and, as such, can be difficult to bin. The best way of dealing with this is to **encourage consumable gifts**. Counter the materialist problem of gift giving by broadcasting hints as to the kind of presents that will go down well around your birthday time: booze, food, socks, handkerchiefs, toiletries, charitable donations ('adopt an octopus'!) and stationery are all perfectly orthodox gifts that can be used or, at the very least, disposed of without raising suspicion. You could also broadcast a strong dislike of novelty gifts like musical ties, plush toys, and crap from the gadget shop. Reciprocate by giving consumable presents to others.

Unless we're talking about something with obvious financial value like a camera or a gold watch, **don't bother selling stuff**. The Japanese word *mendoukusai* means 'more trouble than it's worth'. *Cash in the Attic* and *The Antiques Roadshow* would have you believe that your accumulated junk is worth something. It almost certainly isn't. Give it to a charity shop, Freecycle it (at freecycle.org), leave it on the kerb with a 'Free! Please take!' notice attached, or take it to the tip. The time saved and the expedited rewards of minimalism will far outweigh any pittance you might receive from a sneering assistant at Cash Converters.

There is a tendency to have 'best' and 'everyday' things. This certainly benefits the makers and sellers of things but doesn't really benefit you. You should have **one for 'best' and that's it**. '*Weniger aber besser*', said designer Deiter Rams, or 'less but better'. Dress incredibly well every day. Use your best equipment every day. Eat off the best china and use the best silverware at every meal. Jettison the inferior everyday versions of things and use the best one. You might get hit by a bus tomorrow.

Rather than buying a book, CD, or DVD, **visit your local library**. You're probably only going to read that book once and it might not be worth having on the shelf forever. There's a broader moral here too: consider the advantage of communally owned items over privately owned items. A communally funded facility like a gym or a public library or a bus service is generally better value than the private alternatives. In the case of public services, you're paying for them with your taxes and failure to use them in favour of buying your own things makes you a sucker. Chances are, the people who look after the shared facilities (gym supervisors, librarians, bus drivers) will do a better job than you would. A library card provides access to every book ever written: you probably don't have the means to buy everything yourself. It's also a bit like having staff: why wear yourself out when your team of expert librarians, drivers, and trainers can look after things for you? Generally speaking, **access trumps ownership**.

Shopping is free, my wife says, until you buy something. If you enjoy shopping, **treat shops like museums**. Will owning a thing really help you to enjoy it? A joke overheard is the same as a joke you've paid money to hear. Western culture has an acquisitive bent to it. When we see something appealing we all too often want to own it, to possess it. You'd do well to quash this desire. In particular, if you see some trinket in a shop that takes your fancy, then regard it as you would a museum artefact: appreciate it and move on.

The purpose of getting rid of things is not to make way for more things. Once you've freed space, keep it as space. However, stuff tends to fill the storage space made available to it. Therefore, try to **eliminate storage**

**space** as soon as you have freed it. Once you've cleared a bookcase of old science fiction paperbacks, get rid of the bookcase itself. This will deter you from accumulating more paperbacks.

**Prioritise information over objects**. Japanese architect Kiyonori Kikutake says that 'a Japanese room is determined by information, whereas a Western room relies on objects'. I don't know how true this is but it highlights a distinction between two ideals. Is your home defined primarily by information or objects? Information, even if it's physically manifested as books and CDs, is manageable and can be organised and 'crunched'. This is not possible with objects, which just occupy space without relating to anything. It also helps to highlight the difference between collecting and hoarding.

Above all, **seek experiences rather than things**. Life experiences take up no space and will not weigh you down. Strive to do and to be, not to own. Do you own your possessions or do they own you?

By embracing minimalism – having fun with it, if possible – we can escape consumption. When we escape consumption, we escape work and find ourselves with a lot more free time: 92,000 hours of free time if we completely eliminate our need for jobs and commutes. That's a lot of uninterrupted time to work on your good life projects.

## FRUGALITY (BUT NOT MISERLINESS)

In the first issue of *New Escapologist* a million years ago, we printed a tabular manifesto of things an Escapologist might want to 'escape from' and 'escape to'. It was simplicity itself. One of the things we sought 'escape from' was *miserliness*. Escapologists should not be mean. Leave miserliness to the bureaucrats and worryguts and we shall rejoice and be merry. Don't abstain from pleasure. With time, company, action and thought – give generously.

The same edition of the magazine declared that a key to maintaining a life free of debt and excessive labour is frugality, but this was no contradiction. Frugality doesn't equate to miserliness. Learning to make your own burger patties or to stoke your own wood fire are frugal activities. It would be incorrect to describe them as miserly, since you could feed and warm your friends with such skills. There are many Escapological tools that look like paradoxes but really aren't. Noticing what looks like one is useful warning though: am I being frugal or miserly? Am I an Epicurean or a Puritan? If Bohemianism makes me look cool, is it truly as a consequence of good living or am I courting distinction as a consumer does? The cost of freedom is constant vigilance, or at least an awareness of these potential sinks back into The Trap.

Moreover, frugality need not exclude expensive purchases. You can afford the very finest essentials if you stop buying poor-quality things that need to be replaced all the time (high street clothes and sweatshop shoes) and things that serve only to distract the mind or provide the bare minimum to one's health (computer games, convenience food). The purpose of spending more money on a bespoke suit or the finest whiskies and gins known to science is that the quality is better and so you'll get more out of them. Frugality does not economise on pleasure or quality.

When money is scarce, there are other things with which you can be generous: time, action, company and thought. *Time* is quite abundant when you don't work, so it's easier to be generous with it as a successful escapee. *Action* can be given to assist friends in their projects now that your actions aren't owned by an employer and are therefore yours to give. *Company* in the pub should be spread as widely and inclusively as possible: we might even learn something from the people of other circles. *Thoughts* can be shared freely when you no longer compete with colleagues for managerial affection: commit your unique Escapologist's mind to chewing over other people's problems, offering your Jeeves-like miracle solution at the drop of a hat. Cultivate a generosity of mind and give strangers the benefit of the doubt.

Look for economies of scale to increase the potential for generosity. It's reflexive to baulk at the expense when a round of drinks exceeds a day's income and hard not to feel like a miser for worrying in this way. If, however, you brew five vats of beer in your cellar, you're unlikely to feel the same pinch when it comes to giving it away. How does one resolve frugal behaviour with a pledge against miserliness? Understand the difference between the two; look for opportunities to be generous or hospitable; and be eternally, bountifully bohemian.

## EPICUREANISM

When discussing the good life in Part Two, we talked about Epicurus and his ideas about living well. He favoured simple pleasures, friendship, freedom and thought. Epicureanism is a clear and direct escape from the trap of consumption. We do not need consumption if we learn to appreciate what's there already. Since we must eat, for example, it makes sense to appreciate our food and its preparation. Learning to cook properly instead of relying on pre-prepared meals, fast food, or restaurants can be a great Epicurean pleasure. When we must get from A to B, it makes sense to spend time walking and enjoying the things we see *en route* instead of zooming everywhere in the private bubbles of cars or buses.

Finding free hobbies and interests makes sense. If we can populate our leisure time without relying upon the leisure industries, we can avoid consumption that way too. There are thousands – even millions – of free things to do. You could learn a language, learn computer coding, read books from the library, go for walks, reconnect with nature, volunteer for a charitable organisation, campaign for a political party (vote Green!), go to something on the community calendar, go shopping without buying anything, listen to podcasts, do some press-ups, learn to juggle, hang out with friends or family and *just chat*, look at photographs, have sex, have a wank, do yoga, write a diary, blow spit bubbles, meditate, write poetry, perfect your signature, do handstands, learn the constellations, sleep in a hammock, rearrange the furniture, clean the house and enjoy doing it, watch the clouds go by, or write a time-wasting letter to a Member of Parliament.

When you have free hobbies, you're unlikely to get bored and want to go out and buy things. There's a strong tendency in our consumer society to think that throwing money at a problem will solve it, and that is true of boredom. When we're bored, we think that shopping or paying to see a movie or paying to go on holiday are the solutions: the more money we have, this theory goes, the less likely we are to be bored. Does anyone really think this is true? Does anyone think the lives of millionaires are spent laughing and loving and riding high on the flying elephants ride at Disneyland? Do they live like bonkers lords or like Jeremy Clarkson, buying cars simply to crash them into each other in fits of playful ecstasy, saying 'Hooray! Hooray! I'm in a state of constant satisfaction and I owe it all to my money!'? Of course not.

I suppose now might be a good time to bring up the parable of the Mexican fisherman as a way to think about simple pleasures. It's a bit trite and the kind of thing a school headmaster might bore the kids with in a morning assembly, but the moral is sound:

An American tourist, impressed by the catches of a Mexican fisher-man asks how long it took him to catch such fish. 'Not so long,' says the fisherman. 'What do you do with the rest of your time?' asks the tourist. 'Well,' says the fisherman, 'I rise late, go fishing, play with my children, enjoy the siesta, and then hang out with my friends and my wife and we watch the sun go down.'

'Holy Shit,' says the tourist, corpulent with his own Americanness,

'I'm a business graduate and I can help you to better profit from your time. You should use it to fish more, sell the surplus fish, use that money to buy a bigger house and then you can retire.' Somehow resisting the urge to pull back the American's waistline and empty his bait box into his pants, he asks, 'And then what?' 'Well then,' says the American, 'you can spend your retirement rising late, fishing, and hanging out with your family and your buddies.' He then walks off majestically, wisdom well and truly imparted.

The consumer economy has us working very hard, the eventual reward apparently being a quiet life of simple pleasures. But the quiet life of simple pleasures was there all along. All you had to do was ignore the demands of the consumer economy. You can have the good life now, not later.

The false claim of the consumer economy that a quiet life of contemplation, friendship and gentle naps is only available as some kind of secular afterlife (retirement) is clarified further in Joshua Glenn's *The Wage Slave's Glossary*. Full of etymological wisdom, the book explains the expression 'pie in the sky' as having origins in a unionist song: 'Work and pray, live on hay, / You'll get pie in the sky, when you die'. The idea is that the factory owners (or, for our purposes, the consumer economy) would have us defer even simple pleasures indefinitely, when in fact, as Epicurus suggests, they're almost the whole reason for living. Work and consumption, without simple pleasures, are as good as death.

Embracing Epicureanism allows us to escape consumption because little offered by consumption is compatible with Epicureanism. The hard work required to support a consumerist lifestyle; the expensive, non-simple pleasures; seeing friends and neighbours as competitors: these are opposites of what Epicurus suggests. There is nothing preventing you from embracing Epicureanism this very moment. Decide to love home-baked bread, vegetables, long walks and kissing – instead of Burger King, cars, DVDs, Twitter, and £4 iced coffees. If you're worried that your neighbour thinks you're weird, my advice would be to court it. If that's not your style, invite her over and show her how nice Epicureanism can be.

## ANTI-PRODUCTS

I've got this idea about 'anti-products' as a possible way of breaking the problem of competitive consumption. An anti-product is a unit of empty space, silence, or spareness – that can be bought or sold.

Anti-products already exist and are often positional goods: signs of extreme affluence. It's quite possible that competitive consumption contains the key to its own downfall. Some people, for instance, like to have large apartments and fill them with very little furniture in order to enjoy the peace of empty space. This is an aesthetic choice motivated either by personal taste, or as a form of distinction: 'I'm very Zen,' it says, and 'I've got my shit together'. Moreover, some stressed out go-getters like to spend time (and a lot of money) floating around in sensory deprivation tanks. This involves going inside a soundproof, lightproof tank, usually at a spa, and floating in skin-temperature salt water in near-complete darkness. It is used as a therapeutic escape from stressful modern life. Meanwhile, some artists and writers, if they believe their procrastination problems stem from living in a world of too much noise and too many distractions, will throw up their arms in theatrical despair and go off to sulk and to work on their *magnum opus* (but mainly sulk) at a countryside artists' retreat.

There's nothing to see or do at an artists' retreat or in a sensory deprivation tank, and that's the entire point. People will part with money to experience *less*. This is because empty space, silence and spareness are, to many intents and purposes, the new scarce goods. Opportunities for almost any kind of commercial entertainment are no longer scarce. Physical stuff, manufactured on assembly lines or shat out by magical machines, is no longer scarce, nor are food or water or the other essentials of life. Scarce, however, are opportunities to retreat from all the fun if you want to. Even the reading rooms of public libraries – once havens of studious silence – are now all too often boisterous leisure centres where you're no longer expected to be quiet or even to switch your mobile off. Unless you're a Quaker or you resort to one of the extreme examples of commercially available quietness, it is hard to get a moment's peace.

In a city, we can almost always hear the roar of the traffic. The internet pipes potentially infinite torrents of information into the home (which you could refuse to look at but the temptation to open the laptop lid is often too great to ignore). Everywhere, everything is vying for our attention. The only things we don't have are easy access to empty space, silence, and spareness. This is why people sometimes pay money for them. Whether for therapy, productivity, aesthetic pleasure, or a cool factor, they willingly pay money for *less*. Aside from highlighting what a ridiculous information-heavy consumer culture we've made for ourselves, this also reveals a potential escape from consumption *via* consumption. If we have our hearts truly set on being consumers, we can at least buy or sell something that doesn't destroy the environment or turn the dial even higher on the culture of 'bigger, faster, more violent'.

My advice: if you're rich, buy yourself a city block, empty it of clutter and declare it a silent zone. If this is beyond your means but you still have disposable income, rent an apartment to live in and leave it empty but for the essentials. If you're poor, find a quiet spot in an otherwise busy city and put a clean and empty tent in it.

We can use the logic of competitive consumption against itself. Just as we might (supposedly) look at our neighbour's sports car and feel obliged to compete by getting a better sports car, maybe the neighbour might look to our anti-products as inspiration too. When we refuse to own a car at all and make that decision both clear and appealing through a clean and empty driveway or by converting the garage into something unimaginatively luxurious like a free pub for friends, a beautiful library, or just an empty and silent white space, we might be able to make the Joneses keep up with *us*. Just an idea.

If this is too silly or impractical, the Escapologist should look to do things without an economic imperative. Activities outside the consumer economy, The Trap, will not cost you money or lead to you going back to work. As Thoreau put it: 'beware of all enterprises that require new clothes'. I go one further and suggest caution when any activity requires one to part with money: not out of a desire to be cheap or miserly, but because we should look out for things to do outside of the consumer economy. Soon, we'll find we're immune to the siren song of consumer goods, of upgrades, of fashion, and we will be free to plough our own Escapological furrows.

# 11

# ESCAPE BUREAUCRACY

Tear it into little bits.
— Houdini,
in 'Houdini's Paper Magic:
The Whole Art of Performing with Paper'

## IGNORE IT

Should the non-essential paperwork of some starchy organisation worm its way through your letterbox and plop upon the mat, a useful course of action would be to hold it at arm's length like a bag of dog poo, and then pop it silently into the bin. If they send you an email, delete it and unsubscribe from their mailing list. Even better, don't give them your address in the first place.

Yes, a good way to escape bureaucracy – even *the* bureaucracy – is to ignore it. Insulate yourself to its nagging, petulant, unsolicited whine. 'Treat its commands,' writes anarchist Roderick Long, 'as one would treat the commands of some delusional street person.' Refuse to make eye contact and briskly keep walking. In the event of persistence, smile kindly and offer to buy them a sandwich. It's one of those areas of life where it can pay to be ruthlessly unreasonable. As George Bernard Shaw had it, 'the unreasonable man' is the person who refuses to adapt to society, forcing society to instead adapt to her. 'Therefore all progress depends on the unreasonable man.' It's a good idea. Have you ever noticed that persistently stubborn people usually get what they want in the end? In real life such inflexibility wouldn't make you many friends, but bureaucracy *isn't* real life – it exists in some strange parallel universe of P45s, C72s and APPENDIX 33As – and it was never going to be your friend. It has no face. It can't be befriended or offended. The feelings of a filing cabinet or one of those buff-coloured dossiers with the creepy little string fastener cannot be hurt.

In ignoring paperwork wherever possible, we might even conspire to change the entire bureaucracy. We could be the unreasonable ones upon whom all progress depends. Roderick Long says, 'government is one of the few problems that can be gotten rid of by ignoring it.' Likewise, La Boétie in *Discourse on Voluntary Servitude* suggests it's only our complicity that allows tyrants to get away with tyranny. If enough of us were so unreasonable, the bureaucracy might take note and ultimately make things easier for everyone. There's a growing trend in organisations pushing the time-consuming activities of bureaucracy onto the public instead of taking responsibility for them themselves. It's cheaper for them, but it costs us in time and effort. Paperwork is an imposition and it wouldn't exist in the good life, so let's ignore it wherever possible. It may even be our *duty* as democrats, anarchists, libertarians and (yes) Escapologists to ignore it.

Popping an officious-looking letter into the recycling bin without even deigning to open the envelope can give you quite a thrill. There's no need to fork out on bungee jumping or hard drugs when you can simply discard a scrap of *paper*. And that's all it is, remember. Paper: the same stuff the *Daily Mail* is made of and quite similar to the stuff we use to wipe our bottoms. It's not important. Like the *Mail* itself, it is trivia best ignored. I'd like to think how Kafka's *The Trial* would have gone if Joseph K had completely ignored his arrest and his trial. If he'd treated the arresting officers as Long's 'delusional street people' and got on with celebrating his birthday, he may not have become embroiled in a life-long bureaucratic odyssey. Imagine if you could get special sunglasses like the ones in John Carpenter's *They Live* but instead of revealing the alien invaders around us they rendered bureaucrats as barely-visible, prattling ghosts. We'd probably take them a lot less seriously. Unless there's a genuine threat of going to prison or having your thumbs broken off, treat the world of bureaucracy as if it were a distant land, a Narnia or Bas-Lag populated by ineffective ghosts with only a dim connection to our reality.

## SHUN IT

Bureaucracy plonks down obstacles for Escapologists. Try to set up a business, go self-employed, get planning permission, or put a solar roof on your house and you'll be beset with bureaucracy. I suppose it's there to see how serious you are about your undertaking, which is part of the problem. Why should we be so serious? Can it not be a whim? And whose business is it but our own anyway? One way to deal with this is to go ahead regardless. *Ask for forgiveness, not permission*, the stately Grace Hopper is credited with saying. If you build your shack in the woods without asking, you may have some grovelling to do later but at least you'll be able to do it from the warmth of your shack. Throw your free festival without consulting anyone. It's entirely possible that your guerrilla activity will go unnoticed. If it does get noticed, you can either apologise and move on to the next unsanctioned project or you can protest and appeal. In either event, you'll have enjoyed an experiment in freedom.

A hero of bureaucracy shunning is Chiune Sugihara, a Japanese diplomat based in Lithuania during World War Two. He wrote exit visas for 6,000 Jewish people (putting them through on his signature alone, an act which could have got him and his family executed for treason) because he'd become tired of waiting for Tokyo bureaucracy to get back to him. Sugihara saw the moral imperative to act without permission. Today it is obvious that he did the right thing, but it took superior nerve to snub the authorities in this way and risk being killed for treason. He said, 'some Japanese military leaders were scared because of the pressure from the Nazis; while other officials in the Home Ministry were simply ambivalent. People in Tokyo were not united. I felt it silly to deal with them. So, I made up my mind not to wait for their reply. I knew that somebody would surely complain about me in the future. But I myself thought this would be the right thing to do. There is nothing wrong in saving many people's lives ... The spirit of humanity, philanthropy ... neighbourly friendship ... with this spirit, I ventured to do what I did, confronting this most difficult situation – and because of this reason, I went ahead with redoubled courage.'

We're unlikely to be in a situation quite as grave as Sugihara's, so if he can be the master of his moral domain, so can we in our less life-threatening projects. There's even *fun* to be had in shunning the bureaucracy. I know someone who lives on a canal boat but can't afford the taxes and fees. Periodically, he'll get a note from some agency or other and he enjoys writing back with excuses and moving his boat, even going so far as repainting it, to put them off the scent. Such subterfuge is probably illegal but who cares? Does his liberty harm anyone or cause upset or pollution? No. And then there was the case of the man who 'paid' his electricity bill with a drawing of a seven-legged spider, which he'd 'evaluated' as valuable enough to cover the bill. When the electricity company returned the drawing as unacceptable currency, he responded with 'this cannot be the same spider, for it only has seven legs. I do not believe I would make a mistake like that'. And so it delightfully continued.

In 1974, high-wire artist Philippe Petit walked a tightrope between the towers of the World Trade Centre. The walk was entirely unsanctioned. To complete the feat, Philippe and Co. secured confederates in both towers, to navigate WTC security systems and to find a way of setting up the wire without being detected. The operation was executed with the poise, preparation and secrecy of a heist. *Man on Wire*, the documentary about the caper, has a scene where Petit hides beneath a sheet of tarpaulin while an armed security guard eats a leisurely lunch just feet away. The thrill of the operation was not the wire walk itself but the exhilarating sense of pulling the wool over authority's eyes and doing something unsanctioned. It's the same thrill we get when we see Banksy has left his calling card so spectacularly on the wall of a bank or parliamentary building; when hackers make a mockery of government computer systems; when farmers wake to find impossibly intricate crop circles in their corn field; when urban explorers publish photographs after infiltrating a boarded-up tube station beneath London or Moscow. *Man on Wire* shows a brilliant piece of archive footage of an NYPD cop looking up at Petit's wire in disbelief and wonder. He's thinking, *how?* Mission accomplished. As long as it's ethical, just do what you like. Don't worry too much about the tutting authorities or the finger waggers and the sanctions we never signed up for. It's not our fault we were born into a world of such ridiculous and unnatural rules.

When it comes to paperwork, you could also just leg it. When your life is fairly mobile – something many Escapologists aspire to – it's possible to run away from bureaucracy. It happens naturally whenever you move house. A new flat means all but a new start. This is why you sometimes get paperwork put through the door addressed to a previous tenant: it's paperwork they've escaped and you can put in the bin or return to sender. The 'new start' effect of moving around a lot is also why the authorities hate gypsies and vagabonds so much: people with no fixed address are hard to bureaucratise. Only the most ardent bureaucratic institutions will bother to find out where you've gone. Of course, you could be on a desert island and the Student Loans Company will still find you somehow, perhaps sending you a repayment request by migrating guillemot, so you're probably stuck with them until you can pay off the loan, but the majority of these pain-in-the-arse corporations simply won't bother.

# MINIMISE IT

Minimalism will spring to the rescue in bureaucracy as well as consumerism. We can escape bureaucracy by minimising both our exposure to it and its weight in our lives. You can minimise your exposure to it using some of the avoidance techniques mentioned above. Don't even allow it into your life. But you can also minimise bureaucracy by avoiding the kinds of activities that generate bureaucracy in the first place. Having loads of phones requires bureaucracy. Being on multiple social networking platforms *is* bureaucracy (there's nothing else to it). Having credit cards and multiple bank accounts will generate bureaucracy. Dependence on services and products generates bureaucracy. Find ways to live without these things and hardly any paperwork will come to you. The less of a consumer you are, the less bureaucracy you'll face.

Whenever an email comes to you from some dodgy mailing list, there should be an unsubscribe link. It's worth clicking on, for in a matter of moments you'll have blocked them from troubling you again. If there's no unsubscribe link, set up a filter to run them directly into your trash file or spam box. That'll show 'em. I know it seems like a hassle in the short term to go through the unsubscribe process but it really is worth nipping these minor frustrations in the bud. An ad blocker application will stop pop-ups from crowding your internet-browsing experience and spam filters will stop junk mail coming to your inbox.

And then there's the weight of the admin archive: the box files of old admin squatting in the bottom of closets or filling the drawers of desks. Imagine for a moment that you dislike Christmas decorations as much as you dislike bureaucracy. You might tolerate them at Christmas because it's a social expectation, but it would be absurd to keep them up all year or not to take them down on Twelfth Night. The same can be said for paperwork: by all means keep it while it's relevant or socially necessary, but there's no need to leave it hanging around incessantly. When archiving paperwork, we have a tendency to err on the safe side. There's a fear that if we don't keep every electricity bill and every *communiqué* from the landlord, we'll somehow pay for it later. It doesn't generally happen though. You can ditch almost everything. If your entire paperwork archive was accidentally destroyed, there would probably be one or two inconveniences for you (retrieving forgotten PINs, getting something reissued) but generally speaking you're probably better off without the heft of a paperwork archive in your life.

## MASTER IT

And here's the bad news. For all the fun we can have in ignoring, avoiding or minimising paperwork, there comes a point where it's probably best to master it, to become someone unfazed by paperwork and able to bash it into submission when it arises. I think I'm most depressed when having to humour bureaucracy to enable something quite humble or, worse, something I don't even want to do. I remember completing my UCAS form to get into university at the age of 18. I didn't particularly want to go to university, so the UCAS form was a grinding chore. I was having to apply myself – to act physically and mentally – to facilitate a future event I wasn't particularly interested in. That's like being in debt: you're too deep in the quicksand of obligation, your struggles getting you further from freedom instead of closer to it. I'd suggest applying the avoidance strategy to these projects where you can afford to. Bureaucracy is less unpleasant, however, when it's to facilitate something you're passionate about. If you know that cutting through bureaucracy will benefit you in the long-term or contribute to something worthwhile, it's far less humiliating and frustrating. I recently spent most of a day setting up an international mobile phone to use while travelling. Setting this up proved rather fiddly and precisely the kind of unfreedom I despise, but I found myself patient throughout because I knew that my actions were necessary and directly connected to a personal project. I'd rather have been writing or having fun but knowing that these actions were necessary and relevant took the edge off.

Let's refuse to let admin obstruct the good life or distract us from flow: let's either have a ten minute admin session just before lunch or have an admin day every month or so to take care of it all. Personally, I like to deal with it as soon as it comes in, clubbing each nuisance into oblivion like in a game of whack-a-mole. Occasionally, I'm too efficient. Companies have sometimes sent me reminders about an 'overdue' task because the first reminder is a standard *communiqué*: they can't imagine that I'd dealt with it so quickly. Blam! I sometimes imagine I'm playing a game of *Space Invaders* when dealing with paperwork. Since I hate it, I visualise shooting at a column of advancing Martians. Yes, they're generally getting closer but I can be the Earth's defender. It's surprisingly motivating.

I agree with E. F. 'Small is Beautiful' Schumacher when he wrote: 'We always have to face the simultaneous requirement for order and freedom [...] all real human problems arise from the antinomy of order and freedom [...] Excellent! This is real life, full of antinomies and bigger than logic.' What he means, I suppose, is that some ability to wrangle bureaucracy is a powerful asset for the freedom-seeker. Where we can take control and master bureaucracy, understand the basics of its language and mechanisms, we can be free. It's another example of using The Trap against itself. Just as the Pomodoro Technique (a productivity system in which you work in 25-minute intervals meted out by a kitchen timer) allows you to voluntarily enslave yourself in a 25-minute bubble of self-inflicted unfreedom for the greater personal good, a bit of time spent hacking at bureaucracy can be ultimately liberating. Just be sure that it connects directly to one of your life audit priorities and not to time-wasting trivia. Otherwise, it's best avoided, minimised or snubbed.

# 12

# ESCAPE FROM OUR STUPID, STUPID BRAINS

My brain is the key that sets me free.
— Houdini

## ESCAPE BAD FAITH
## BY EMBRACING FREE WILL

The key to escaping Bad Faith – the fear of acknowledging a reality of infinite choices – lies in learning to embrace freedom, life beyond The Trap, properly. Humans have *motility*: the physical ability to move from one place to another. It's one of our most valuable assets and we don't usually appreciate it until it's taken away by some horrible accident or through accidentally locking ourselves in the garage. Motility is what people and dogs and raccoons usually have but plants and mushrooms and sea anemones do not. Some appliances are stuck to a mains socket, others have batteries. To deny you're one of the battery gang is to exhibit Bad Faith, to squander one of your finest assets. You don't have to stay in the same place forever if you don't want to.

To embrace motility instead of denying it, it helps to prove to yourself that motility is both possible and not to be feared. As we said earlier, this can be daunting. Do the fear setting exercise described in Chapter 8, but also exercise your motility as often as possible. Just as the exercise of muscle in the gym or exercise of the mind in *Sudoku* or a leisurely game of chess will enhance those facilities, exercise of motility should likewise enhance *that* facility and to escape Bad Faith. You could do this through travel, by visiting foreign places, seeing them with your own eyes and appreciating the fact that you went there under your own steam. If you visit Istanbul, appreciate that you did so through your own actions: you may not have walked every step of the way, but you booked the flights from your computer and picked up the *lira* at the currency exchange and lined up for a visa at Atatürk airport. You weren't whisked away by God or cajoled into going there by some company or group or authority figure. You went there through exercising your own free will – your motility – and thereby defeating Bad Faith *once*. Each time you exercise motility, you act with free will.

If long-distance travel is not your cup of tea, you could exercise free will through walking. Walk whenever you can. If you can walk to work, take different routes as often as possible. You'll find yourself taking note of new sights – a rickety-looking fire escape you've not seen before, an architectural flourish, a clothes line strung between buildings – all of which will contribute in a small but cumulative way to a sense of perspective. Know that you saw those things and pushed the boundaries of your experience using your own free will and not because somebody told you to. If you have time, take walks purely for leisure. Walk through neighbourhoods you've no business in. Walk through the lobbies of hotels you're not staying in. Walk at night when everyone else is in bed. Walk through your neighbourhood around 6pm and look at people tossing crepes or pulling roasts from ovens through their illuminated kitchen windows. These experiences – these minor trespasses – add up. They lead to proving to the fearful, greedy caveman brain that anywhere can be explored through simple acknowledgement of motility and will.

Strange things happen when you go walking, actually. There's something about the rhythm and the silence that leads you to think along certain lines. You end up solving problems and reaching conclusions.

Activist and 'naked rambler' Stephen Gough, known for being arrested every five minutes for nude hillwalking, once said, 'I wasn't working. I spent my time looking after the kids and going for walks. One day I was walking and something happened. I realised I was good. Being British, buried in our upbringing is that we're not good or have to watch ourselves – maybe it comes from religion, or school. I realised that at a fundamental level I'm good, we're all good, and you can trust that one part of yourself.' Gough is right. You are good. You're not a human resource for someone else to exploit or push around. But you need to banish Bad Faith to come to a conclusion like that.

You can also exercise free will by embarking upon a completely self-initiated project: by doing something (anything at all) that you've chosen for yourself instead of being suggested to you by a boss or a family member or someone else with a vested interest in how you live. Build a tree house. Take a course. Spend Sunday mornings picking up litter on your street. Learn to skip rope. Take up fencing. Learn a not-entirely-useful language like Sanskrit or Navajo or Klingon. Set up a fan website to some obscure musician or artist who won't have been expecting it. The further away the activity from your day-to-day *modus operandi*, the more powerful and convincing it will be.

Remember that you're not doing this to make an impression on anyone else. You're doing it to make an impression *on yourself*, to prove to yourself that acting outside of the prescribed lines is both possible and rewarding, to blow away the superstitions and doubts. The more we prove to ourselves that free will is real and can be acted upon, the less likely we are to be seduced by the apparent but illusory safety of Bad Faith.

## ESCAPE ANXIETY

There's some truth in the idea that if you act in a certain way, your actual mood will shift in the same direction, as if to rationalise your behaviour after the fact. 'Smile and you'll feel happy,' being the commonest (and most irritating) way of expressing this. I find that if I shrug my shoulders, make a farting sound in the side of my mouth, say 'Oh, so what?', or immediately start doing press-ups or eating sweets instead of tackling a problem, I start to care less about it. And then it stops being a problem. This is, in fact, a lesson with roots in Stoicism. We should train ourselves to stop seeing problems as problems. We can't control everything in the world but we can control the perception they leave in our brains. Obviously, this can't always work for real problems. When finding a worrying lump, the best course of action is probably to visit a doctor. When a football comes crashing through the window, it's probably a good idea to put up some cling film and call a glazier. But even in cases like these, a shrug of the shoulders can help to diffuse some of the stress. Some problems aren't really problems at all once stress is removed from the equation, and the real problems – the worrying lumps and broken windows – can be met head-on with a cool head. Act like you care less, and maybe you'll feel as if you really do care less. If you're not naturally inclined to nonchalance, channel one of your cooler friends as I do with Mr Money Mustache. Better still, get a hammock. It'll be the best £25 you'll ever part with. Nothing – save perhaps a careless neighbour edging toward your guy ropes with a pair of garden shears – seems terribly problematic from a hammock. Just watch the clouds broiling above you, smashing to bits and reforming in the sky. Eat a peach. Blow smoke rings. Have a soak in the bath.

## ESCAPE INFORMATION ANXIETY

This just in: the end is not nigh. A couple of years ago, I started feeling nervous on planes. Where I used to feel liberated at take-off, I'd begun having thoughts about mechanical faults and sabotage and terrorism and how flight is even possible in this world of malfunctioning toasters anyway. This was bad news for me because not only do I live between Scotland and Canada but travel is an item on my life audit. I wondered where this fear could possibly have come from. It was new. I never feared flying before.

Well, it came from the news obviously. 'What the eyes see and the ears hear,' said Houdini, 'the mind believes,' which is precisely why newspapers make us feel nervous all the time. The unforgettable images of 9/11 speak directly to the caveman brain and so do the news stories of commercial planes falling out of the sky, all lives lost or simply never found again. I salved my concerns a little by telling myself that I'd rather die in a plane crash – an adventurer's death! – than in some pointless domestic balls-up like slipping on a bath mat or being incinerated by a chip pan. If there turns out to be an afterlife it would be really embarrassing. Besides, the odds of plane crash death are extremely, extremely tiny. Riding in cars is far more dangerous. In a great book called *Risk* by Dan Gardner the author points out that more people died after 9/11 because of choosing to drive instead of catching flights, than died in the actual event. But, as Gardener points out, these facts do not appeal to caveman brain and thus don't feel as real somehow. Overcoming the fears of the caveman brain is never easy, especially in a relatively strange situation like being shot into the sky in a metal tube while trying to hold in a wee until the seat belt light says it's okay to go.

Joseph Heath in his dazzling book *Enlightenment 2.0* explains that the solution to this problem is to create a more *rational* environment. If it's a struggle to use our primitive brains to think rationally, the creation of a less hysterical environment should help. The news media, he says, ought to be less sensational, biased and salacious than they currently are. Alas, news media are sensational, biased and salacious because their primary goal seems to be to make money and to maintain a status quo rather than to dispassionately inform. Until we succeed in properly regulating news media, this isn't going to change. In the meantime, I say, we can insulate ourselves to it. Let's stay away from the shocking images, the hate speak and the fearmongering of the news. Planes do not generally fall out of the sky. Thousands of planes fly safely every day. You can see them criss-crossing the skies, straight and true, just by looking up.

We need to maintain a healthy information diet, to control the information that flows into our heads. You are what you think, and information dictates your thoughts. Luckily, we can replace most of the manic junk information of news media with information worth consuming. Instead of haunting the news websites or watching the television news, let us read books, listen to music, go somewhere to enjoy live entertainment like theatre or stand-up comedy or live music. We don't need to fear missing out. We'll still find out about things through no action of our own. The main radio station I listen to, BBC 6 Music, despite being dedicated to music, has a two-minute news bulletin every hour; headlines foist themselves on us from the sidebars of websites or from the free papers lying around in train stations; and, of course, people still talk. Let's avoid junk information from newspapers and social networks, and favour (if anything) long form journalism from good-quality magazines like *The New Yorker*, *Jacobin* and *Aeon*. More than anything, let's read books: proper, well written books to properly inform, to help lift the spirits and the soul soar. Better still, let's go out for a walk and see what the real world's up to: there won't be any images of charred fuselage to set your amygdala sparking when you're outdoors and people-watching or looking at moss instead.

It's probably wise to minimise our exposure to social media. Even if we don't buy a newspaper or hit up the *Guardian* website very often, news items will find their way into our newsfeeds or into the trending sidebars. These items, of course, will always be the most sensational. (Typical example: I followed a link to a perfectly innocuous *Huffington Post* article today. An unrelated sidebar headline reads, 'The Moon Could, Theoretically, Hit the Earth'.) Facebook is the worst offender for this and I'd advise anyone to quit it. Twitter's not so bad so long as you resolutely follow a small number of people. Needless to say, Reddit and BuzzFeed (or whatever their equivalent may be when you read this) are best not touched with a ten-foot pole. Treat these websites as gorgon heads: one quick peek and turn to stone. And if you really want to commit to a healthy information diet, perhaps madam would consider overarming her mobile phone into the river? With a single *ploop!* we can be free of that much.

## ESCAPE STATUS ANXIETY

Alain de Botton in his great book *Status Anxiety* offers five solutions to its titular problem: philosophy, art, Christianity, politics and Bohemia. I can very well get behind three of those. (The jury's still out on politics and I'll only entertain a religious solution if it happens to be voodoo). The greatest of these, in my opinion, is Bohemia.

The philosopher William James was concerned with the problems of social standing and he offers us the equation that Self-esteem = Success ÷ Expectation. In other words, to think well of yourself you can either become more successful or you can lower your expectations. Unfortunately, the former requires a lot of miserable striving or a lot of luck, and the latter is unappealing to most people because every message echoing in the cavernous hallways of The Trap says that lowering one's expectations is a bad thing, that we should strive and reach ever higher. What The Trap doesn't tell us is that the whole arrangement is bogus. By definition, it's impossible for us *all* to occupy the higher echelons of society. Meritocracy is a pyramid scheme. Reaching for the top is a fool's errand. Asian-American thinker Lin Yutang says there are three observable 'humbugs' of life – wealth, fame and power – but that 'there is a convenient American word which again combines these three humbugs into one: success'. He says, 'The price [of success] is often very heavy… the strenuousness of a presidential campaign alone is enough to frighten off all the wise souls of America. A public office often demands that a man attend six dinners a week in the name of consecrating his life in the service of mankind. Why does he not consecrate himself to a simple supper at home and to his bed and his pajamas?'

Besides, look at the people who tend to occupy the ranks of the successful. Business people like Donald Trump and Cherie Blair; moguls like Rupert Murdoch; seedy pillars of the entertainment establishment like Jimmy Savile; career politicians like David Cameron and Tony Blair. Why would anyone want to join *them*? The upper echelons seem populated by dullards, tyrants and paedos. I'm willing to entertain that some upper echelon types might have been good people once but are morally withered, essentially corrupted by the clamber to the top or the company they end up keeping. Better, one might suggest, to be humble. This doesn't mean defeat or mediocrity. You could be a wise, happy and spiritually fulfilled janitor in the heart of the good life. Be Epicurus. Be Lin Yutang. Be the Mexican fisherman.

The illusion of meritocracy offered by The Trap makes wealth look almost like moral superiority. It's not. Trump and the others are not better than the rest of us for occupying those higher echelons. There's no reason to aspire to be like them. We know it, but we keep striving anyway, perhaps because we don't want the *top* echelon but just the *next* one so we can lord it over the people who were once our peers. And there lies our solution: to *stop climbing* because there will always be another echelon and before you know it you've stepped on a snake and slid to the bottom again or (worse) you actually succeed and have to rub shoulders with the likes of Donald Trump.

So how can we learn to be happy with our place on the meritocratic pyramid? How can we escape status anxiety? I believe the answer lies in Alain de Bottom's fifth solution: Bohemia. Bohemia is a threadbare but vibrant utopia in which one can prioritise creativity, love, merriment, experimentation and arousal of the senses. Bohemians can be found throughout the nineteenth century (Baudelaire, van Gogh, The Romantics) and twentieth century (the Dadaists, Jack Kerouac, the Bloomsbury Group, Augustus John, William S. Burroughs, George Orwell in Paris and London, the Punks) and certainly in the present day (me, baby). Let's be Bohemians! If we deliberately divorce ourselves from bourgeois status symbols – cars, employment, brand names, newspapers – it no longer feels like failure when we're not consuming the best examples of these things. We'll spend less energy keeping up with the Joneses and eventually leave status anxiety behind forever.

The Bohemian can come from almost any walk of life: she can be male or female, rich or poor and from any ethnic background. What Bohemians universally share is rejection of the ideals of the bourgeois. Comfort and security are all well and good, but not at the cost of liberty, love and lustiness. The Bohemian knows that money, property and status have little to do with the content of one's character, and that professional success and widespread celebration have little to do with talent. Of value to the Bohemian is spiritual integrity and creative freedom. The Bohemian would sooner live in poverty than submit to an undesirable job.

This belief in integrity and an intense desire for creative freedom can lead to a threadbare existence. Perhaps this material poverty (or 'simplicity' as Thoreau would call it) leads to the archetypal Bohemian, wild at heart and empty of pocket. When you're a Bohemian, you simply don't care any more about status or relative wealth. The Bohemian is unlikely to suffer status anxiety because she plays a wholly different game.

An advantage of the Bohemian life is that it's, by necessity, cheap. It costs little to engage in Bohemian pursuits. You don't need to save up lots of money to enter Bohemia and you don't even need to have regular income. You can begin today by turning down the volume on the bourgeois command system in your brain. By living cheaply – by lowering your overheads to the absolute minimum – you can probably afford to work part-time instead of full-time or put less stress on your cottage industry.

Bohemians help society simply by living. Alain de Botton says, 'It's one of the cheering things about Bohemia, that people who set out simply to live as they choose often end up winning great freedom for everyone. Many of the freedoms we now take for granted – to talk to whom we like, to have relationships with whom we like, not to have to wear a hat in public, even to put garlic in our food – were first established in Bohemia.' Let's live as Bohemians. Let's grow our hair, ignore the values of the rat race, shed our anxieties and be free.

## ESCAPE EXISTENTIAL ANXIETY

In a world where death is the only real certainty, it might seem that existential anxiety is inescapable. In fact, death's inevitability is a rather good clue about how to abolish it. Knowing you're not going to be here forever should be a relief: knowing there's a way out means you don't have to worry about how important you are or whether there's a God or if you have a destiny. Know instead that you're only here for 100 years at best, that it's too short a time to come up with any definite answers and hang up your fretting beret once and for all.

This is why Bohemians of the nineteenth century were so fond of skulls: a human skull (a plaster one usually) sitting on a shelf among your books is a reminder that life is temporary and too fleeting to be spent fretting. It's a *memento mori*: a reminder of your mortality can be the solution to existential anxiety. Get yourself a skull, read something by Caitlin Doughty, go to an archaeological museum (or a dig), hang out with some Goths. If, however, you don't like to think about death all the time I suggest this: contemplate the cosmos. Or if that's too outrageous and spiritual sounding for your liking, contemplate the various forms of life in the very deep sea. Either way, it has the effect of pulling your consciousness far, far away from your problems.

Your place in the world doesn't actually matter that much when you learn to see it from the outside. Does it matter that a piece of dust somewhere in your house is positioned imperfectly? Does the *feng shui* of dust concern you? Of course it doesn't. And when you begin to think about the impossibility of the cosmos or the machinations of barrel-eyed fish in the very deep sea, your existential anxieties will seem precisely like the *feng shui* of dust.

I'm fond of asking myself 'What would the "Wise Space Baby" make of all this?' The Wise Space Baby is the gigantic and mysterious creature who appears at the end of *2001: A Space Odyssey*. I think the proper name of the creature is actually the 'Star Child' but I find that name quite mawkish and creepy, so I like to call it the Wise Space Baby instead. The Wise Space Baby is up there *right now*, seeing all. He's not God or even a god. He's a baby. But he's wise and lives somehow in space. He's probably eternal. He's something to do with the epic scale of the human story and the impossibility of the vastness of the universe. One thing's for sure, he finds even your biggest problems pretty charming.

Worrying about our place in the universe is absurd. If you doubt this, try to imagine how things must look from the greatest of great heights or the deepest of depths. What would Zeus think of our attempts at civilisation? What would the creatures of the Marianas Trench think of them? Even the astronauts on the International Space Station have come to some pretty damning conclusions about what humans get up to and they're only 200 miles up. To the cosmic outsider, the international and historic sum of our malcoordinated human activity must seem offensively stupid or, at best, cute. To the Wise Space Baby or Zeus or Cthulhu, our civilisation must look like a macaroni Mother's Day card. Any ambitions held by creatures as limited, short-sighted, mortal, and quaint as ourselves would look very, very silly when viewed from on high. This is how we reach that Woody Allen joke: How do you make God laugh? Tell Him your plans. You came from nothing, you'll leave with nothing. Have fun while you're here. 'Life is Absurd,' says Tom Hodgkinson: 'Be Merry be Free'.

## ESCAPE STRESS

I have a degree in psychology – from the University of Wolverhampton no less – and I can remember the lectures about stress quite clearly. I was struck by how obvious it all was. The actual facts about stress and stress reduction techniques were pretty humdrum, the solutions tantamount to old wives' tales: meditate, keep a diary, feed the birds. Of particular entertainment value was something called the Holmes and Rahe Stress Scale: a list of life events ranked in order of stressfulness, from 'death of spouse' (worth 100 stress points) to 'Christmas' (worth 12). Along the way there were items like 'trouble with in-laws' (29) and 'sexual difficulties' (39) and, interestingly, many of the life stressers were events that are supposed to make us happy like 'marriage' (50), 'vacation' (13), and even 'outstanding personal achievement' (28). How strange we humans are: we stress about getting somewhere and once we're there we find it stressful. You'd be forgiven for wanting to go back to bed and stay there indefinitely in some kind of padded hat, only that might result in a stressful 'change of sleeping habits' (16). We're so damn delicate.

For some perverse reason, I tried to imagine all of the events of the Holmes and Rahe Stress Scale happening to one hapless man in a single day, getting married but his partner dying while on vacation and having to give the news to his new in-laws, his head finally exploding over Christmas dinner. I think I found it entertaining because I was a precocious undergraduate, rather full of myself, with no intention of doing anything so stoutly bourgeois as getting married or celebrating Christmas or achieving anything outstanding or otherwise. But in my puerility, I happened upon the most effective form of stress avoidance: avoid stressful situations. If we don't go around getting married, taking out loans, or having babies, we won't experience so much stress. The solution to 'trouble with boss' (23) will also be clear to the Escapologist. The responsibility-avoiding Bohemian, then, can expect to live to a ripe old age without a single furrow of worry. Of course, it's possible these stressers are worth it: parents might find eventually that the compensations of family – companionship, bonding, pride, hope for the future – outweigh the stress of it. But know that it's a choice. One doesn't necessarily have to take on all (or any) of these challenges. It is not cowardly or naff or selfish to say no thanks. We usually, like it or not, have a choice.

The Escapologist, of all people, can expect to avoid stress most easily simply by virtue of her lifestyle. If you don't have a job, a daily commute, too much work to do, an irritating mobile phone, a Twitter reputation to court, and too much physical stuff to manage, you're unlikely to face so much stress. If you do have a job and a daily commute and all the other things you'd like one day to escape, simply having an actionable escape plan will help to reduce stress: it will give you an idea of how far you must go in terms of time and energy to reach the end of your struggle. Having goals and plans can help to eliminate stress. As an Escapologist, you have the results of your life audit to inform these. You only have a certain amount of time in a week – the same amount of time as anyone else – and you can fill it precisely how you'd like to: the life audit shows you the direction you should be moving in, so you can create goals and plans (with properly thought-out dates and outcomes) based on this.

Minimalism can help too. (There's no such thing as therapeutic minimalism, so far as I know, but I've made it up now – so let us all rejoice in this new emerging science.) Sometimes, if I'm feeling stressed, I get rid of something: I delete some stuff from my hard drive or jettison a few items from my wardrobe, and revel in the post-puke euphoria that comes from lightening the load. A benefit of minimalism is that it allows you to exert control over your surroundings. Stress happens when you feel out of control, so by proving to yourself that you can exert control in one area (e.g. your hard drive, wardrobe or CD rack) you can reduce the anxiety you might be experiencing over something else. One of my favourite things to minimise if I'm ever feeling stressed, is my admin file. I pull out a few old telephone bills or job contracts, tear them up and throw them away. Life is better with less paperwork in it. By reducing stress in that area, I can move on to tackle stress in the area of most concern.

## ESCAPE EGO

Ego can be escaped by redefining your heroes. Heroes offered by The Trap usually appeal to our egos: rock stars, athletes, hugely popular entertainers. It does this in order to perpetuate the myth of the meritocracy. If you worked hard and bought the right things, it says, you could be like Robbie Williams or Venus Williams or Prince William(s).

Unfortunately, it's a myth. People who 'make it' usually have tremendous advantages over the rest of us and don't usually arrive on the higher echelons of society through hard work or clever consumption at all. Those who do transcend are rare examples and appeal to the caveman brain in a similar way to those 9/11 aeroplane photographs: as powerful anecdotal evidence that an unlikely thing could really happen to us. Statistically, we don't have much chance of becoming super-successful or being plunged into oblivion by terrorists but the caveman brain sees the example and freaks out about it. Just as we might become nervous flyers, we might also become aspirational.

This is a problem because it can lead to a squandered life of unnecessary struggle. The way around it is to give the ego something else to occupy itself with. We should restructure our hero pantheon to include people of integrity. This will still appeal to the ego but it won't lead to problems. If you aim to be like Augustus John, Vanessa Bell or Virginia Woolf – the Bohemians – it's not only attainable but rewarding. Among my heroes are the comedian and actor Daniel Kitson for creating consistently excellent work and doing everything he can to avoid celebrity status; Penny Rimbaud and Gee Vaucher for sticking to their values after being in a prominent punk band; my Nan for living with a threadbare, fun-loving kind of dignity; and Woody Allen for creating a film each year even when they're clearly based on ideas previously used on *The Flintstones*. From this a new type of 'success' emerges. Yes, it might very well be necessary to become hipsters.

We shouldn't exile the ego completely; but we should re-point it in more interesting and more achievable directions. I suppose this is what William James might have meant about lowering our expectations in order to find self-esteem (Self-esteem = Success ÷ Expectation). The ego can be satisfied without necessarily high rock star or tycoon-level expectations. Again, Bohemia offers a solution. I'd rather be a vain Bohemian than a vain and exhausted failure or even a vain success story. Which is lucky really.

# ESCAPE DEPENDENCIES

Yemeni traders, as an aide to productivity and as an on-the-go indulgence, might chew *Qat* leaves. The effects are something like those of drinking coffee. *Qat* is a stimulant and known to result in a mild psychological dependency. To be cut off from one's supply of the leaf is to be haunted by the demon *Katou*. We've all known *Katou* or something like him. Seldom are we completely free of vice (nor would we want to be) and, where there's vice, there is, inevitably, *Katou*. The Escapologist – someone who actively seeks pleasure – must be vigilant when it comes to keeping *Katou* out. We must minimise our dependencies. A dependency is a cost. It's another obstacle between us and freedom, a complication the Escapologist can do without.

To escape dependencies, we must first identify them. Mine include coffee and sugar. Make a little list. Or a big list. Now you can have fun with eliminating them. The practice of Neuro-linguistic Programming (NLP) offers ways to overcome habits. Here's *New Escapologist's* eudaemonology editor (yes, we have one of those) Neil Scott to explain:

> Neurologically speaking, consciousness is a joke, capable of processing only seven bits of information per second. The unconscious can processes fourteen million bits of information per second, which is why we should look there to explain our actions. Addictions (even relatively soft ones, like caffeine and computer games) are compelling because they leverage the full weight of the unconscious mind. Our associations with these things stimulate all the main senses: sight, sound, touch, smell and taste. NLP, unlike other therapeutic practices, speaks directly to the unconscious. It compels people to evoke the addictive sensation and then

reduce its hold over the mind via simple techniques, like "The Swish", which help to change associations.

To Swish:

– identify the negative behaviour (e.g. drinking coffee).
– imagine how you want to feel instead (e.g. a clear-headed, super-focused Buddha-like figure)
– find the trigger for the negative behaviour (e.g. the coffee flowing, strong and black from the pot to your favourite mug)
– swish between the two images (e.g. visualise the coffee pot image being pushed into the background while bringing the Zen-master image to the foreground)

That was Neil Scott, ladies and gentlemen. We once went to a music festival together and he never touched an illicit substance the whole time we were there, if you don't count *falafel*. Mind like a fortress.

Once you've eliminated a dependency, you can occasionally indulge. In the Jim Jarmusch film *Coffee and Cigarettes*, Tom Waits and Iggy Pop enjoy a cigarette to celebrate that they no longer smoke. 'The beauty of quitting,' says Tom, 'is that now that I've quit, I can have one.' It's funny and contains an element of truth. If you're no longer under the cosh of addiction, you can enjoy these pleasures occasionally and properly. The key, I find, is not to completely abstain from all pleasures, but to become a master of them. Call upon your pleasures when you see fit: not when the *Katou* sets in.

## ESCAPE THE BRAINS OF OTHERS

There will always be people, those still trapped and those who benefit from The Trap, who want to pull you back in. Not only must we escape our own caveman brains but also those of others. They want us back for theirs because the well-meaning among their number fear for us and because the malign among them want to juice us for money and energy and zest.

In *Coming Up for Air*, Orwell's narrator lives in near-hysterical fear of these others: 'All the soul-savers and Nosey Parkers, the people whom you've never seen but who rule your destiny all the same, the Home Secretary, Scotland Yard, the Temperance League, the Bank of England, Lord Beaverbrook, Hitler and Stalin on a tandem bicycle, the bench of bishops, Mussolini, the Pope. I could almost hear them shouting: "There's a chap who thinks he's going to escape! There's a chap who says he won't be streamlined! He's going back to Lower Binfield! After him! Stop him!"'

In reality, there are family and friends and former colleagues who would have us back in the clutches of The Trap. They advised us against quitting our jobs, or at least treated it with suspicion or contempt. Even after years of proving to them that another life is possible, they'll still want to pull us back in. Perhaps it's their own sadness – their own desperation to believe that their lives are the best lives – that motivates them, or perhaps they're genuinely concerned for our marbles and they'd rather we return to the bosom of mediocrity than end up being kidnapped at a petrol station and buried alive by a sociopath while trying to hitch-hike to Bruges. It's not unreasonable of them. We're choosing danger and it concerns them. Or specifically, it concerns their caveman brains. Some of their tribe has gone loco and they want to reel us back in to safety. The best thing to do, I think, is to assure them soberly and rationally that our decisions are our own and we'll gladly return to the rat race should authentic trouble rear its head. Ultimately, we cannot live our lives for other people.

Above all, in escaping the quirks of psychology seized upon and exploited by The Trap, we must overrule the caveman brain: that unreliably old-fashioned internal adviser. Perhaps 'overrule' is too cruel a word – it's not the fault of the caveman brain that it's been cast asunder in our magnificent, gliding futureworld – so perhaps 'soothe' is the best word or 'mollify'. We need to show the poor caveman within that there's nothing to fear anymore: there's plenty to eat, our tribes are at peace, the sabre-toothed tigers all long gone.

# THE POST-ESCAPE LIFE

*When I passed back his irons, he grinned at me and said,*
*'I don't know how you did it, but you did!' and*
*he shook me cordially by the hand.*
*— Houdini*

## QUESTIONS

So you're free. The walls of The Trap have faded away. You've done it. You've applied your willpower and you've escaped. Rejoice! Have another cigar. Eat another peach. If you want to, that is. Nobody can tell you what to do now.

It's important, however, to review our situation every now and then, even in freedom. It prevents us from slipping back into The Trap. Does your world look like the freedom you imagined before escaping? How much, if at all, does it differ from your vision? Does this imperfection matter? Do you *feel* free or are your new habits a new kind of trap? If so, how can you escape them? Are you content with this sensation of constant vigilance? If not, how can you escape *that*? Is your current world sustainable or do you still feel as if you're on a miniature treadmill? Houdini's posters claimed that 'nothing on Earth can hold Houdini a prisoner': can you make that claim about yourself yet? Would you be comfortable putting it on your posters?

It's a constant process. You may be free now, but Escapology is a constant practice and you mustn't stop practising. Are you working too hard in your cottage industry or your creative practice? If so, incorporate some strict hammock time into your schedule. Understand that it's as important as any act of industry.

The most terrifying (and therefore most important) question that will haunt any successful Escapologist is this: Have I *really* escaped? Is it possible that The Trap allowed me to *think* I escaped, but I'm actually in a special annex reserved for clever dicks and not free at all? We must exercise our free will daily, hourly, constantly. We must learn to tell the difference between free will and obligation. That is how we'll know.

## KEEP HUMAN!

It must be a lot easier to be an agoraphobe than it used to be. From the dawn of time up until about 1997, it was really very important to leave the house sometimes lest you starve to death. These days, you could conceivably never leave the house at all. You could stay in a single tiny room if you liked. All business can be conducted online, making stock trades or freelancing as a copywriter to make money, Skyping with clients, and having groceries delivered via home shopping websites. It would be easy-peasy. I wonder if there are any Kaspar Hauser-type people out there who simply never, ever come outdoors. I don't know any, but obviously they're out there. Or rather, in there.

As a writer, it could easily happen to me. There have been times I've not left the house for something like three days if I've had work to do or I've just been too bone idle or if the Montreal weather has been particularly insane. As efficient as it would be to get through an entire day on a single calorie, it would be a singularly wretched existence, never seeing the sky or rubbing shoulders with other people. In fact, it would probably suit the proponents of The Trap down to the ground, for us all to be safely tucked away in our claustrospheres, never going out and never raising hell.

Despite not being drawn to read a single one of his novels, I use

Henry Miller's 'eleven commandments' for writers (originally just for himself, but later included for insight in his *On Writing* book). It's all sensible advice along the lines of 'work on one thing at a time until finished', but my favourite commandment is 'keep human!' He knew very well of the dangers of becoming a lonely, bearded shut-in with body odour that could melt an anvil. 'Keep human!' he said, 'see people, go places, drink if you feel like it.'

He also said 'don't be a draught horse! Work with pleasure only,' which is also important. It's best to only work when it results in pleasure. Amusingly, Francesco Cirillo, who came up with the Pomodoro Technique admits, 'the main disadvantage of the Pomodoro Technique is that to reach your goals effectively, you need to accept being helped by a little mechanical object.'

When I read over the short chapters in my last book, I can tell exactly which ones were written with pleasure and which ones I had to bang out of my unwilling brain because of a deadline or a self-imposed attempt at discipline. I daresay the readers can tell too, so without pleasure the work is compromised. And, after all, what's the point of escaping one daily grind in an office somewhere only to build your own self-inflicted daily grind at home? The location may be preferable and there's no commute, but you're still a slave. The entire point of escaping work is to maximise pleasure and to reduce pain. This is what I mean when I talk about 'the terrible question' of 'have I *really* escaped?'

'Don't be nervous,' said Miller, 'work calmly, joyously, recklessly, on whatever is in hand.' It's up to you to create an environment in which you can work with pleasure as much or as little as you please, and to always 'keep human' by going out sometimes, getting drunk and singing. You can go back to your cottage industry when the bar staff beg you to leave.

# NEVER FORGET

Occasionally, in my post-escape life, I'll find myself on a bus during rush hour. It's usually by accident because I'll have no idea what time it is, but it serves as a kind of *memento mori*, a good way of remembering my potential fate. Such accidental crossing paths with the yet-to-escape, makes you extremely grateful for the freedom in which you now find yourself. Maybe we should declare an annual 'international emancipation day' (March 24th for Houdini's birthday perhaps?) when successful Escapologists the world over set their alarm clocks for 7am and pile onto rush hour trains and buses. It would remind us all of how bad things used to be.

It's vital that we never forget the clock-watching, the commutes, the fire drills, the unsuitable working environments, the mindless submission, the fact that it's so hard to get into a leisurely frame of mind when recovering from a day's work when we're at home or with friends in the evening. Never forget the petty office politics, the cross-business politics, the early rises, the pointless meetings, the flickering screens, the fluorescent lighting. When you're sitting in the park on a summer's day or holed up against a log fire in midwinter; planning one of your own rewarding projects or soaking in the bath thumbing through *Brideshead Revisited*, spare a thought for your self in the past or the parallel universe version of yourself who never tried to escape and know that escape was the right decision.

# AFTERWORD:

# SEVEN BILLION ESCAPOLOGISTS,

## OR

# WHAT IF EVERYONE DID THIS?

*Eventually he managed to secure his freedom,
and, breathing free air once more …
he silently folded his tent and stole away.*
*— Houdini*

At the heart of this book is a simple truth: it is our natural state to be free. We have minds capable of decision-making and imagination. We have arms and legs or prosthetic equivalents allowing us to act. As if this weren't enough, we occupy a moment in history in which – however it may seem to the contrary – we are free to walk away from obligations without fear of very serious reprimand. As with Milgram's experiment, the door is open and we can leave at any time we like. A voice of authority might say 'the experiment requires that you continue' but we have the power to ignore it and we always did. We are each in possession of an independent will and, so long as it's morally upheld, it's our pleasure and duty to act upon it.

To escape The Trap today is a personal decision. It requires no major change of political regime and no need to change the cultural consciousness. We do not need to become activists or utopians or to wait for a climate more conducive to pursuit of the good life to come along. It's not a trend, not quite a lifestyle: it's *ethics*, a way of looking at the world and at life. It's a simple conversion of commonly held values and priorities into uncommon ones, a value shift from which action will inevitably follow. Perhaps more than anything, it's about our time on Earth and choosing how to spend it. It's about taking control of our circumstances rather than outsourcing that control to others.

A common objection to a life of freedom is that if everyone acted as Escapologists, it would all fall apart; that our consumer economy must be served and for this a slave caste is both necessary and right. It's nonsense. It's an objection based on the assumption that to be free is to freeload, which is not necessarily the case. It's an outwardly projected version of the very fear that keeps so many people punching the clock. It sides with the bourgeois terror of instability over the Bohemian values of integrity, equity, adventure, courage and personhood.

This being said, the objection contains a useful question. It's old-fashioned, but asking 'what if everyone did this?' is a good ethical yardstick. It can help to differentiate between an act of selfish deviance and one of useful dissent. Asking 'what if everyone did this?' leads to statements like:

> If everyone were to drop litter, our cities would be messy. Therefore littering is an act of selfish deviance.

> If everyone were to boycott the *Daily Mail*, it would cease to be printed and we'd all be better off for it. Therefore boycotting the *Mail* is an act of useful dissent.

So what if everyone lived like an Escapologist? I suppose we'd have to find a new word to start with. We wouldn't be 'Escapologists' if the status quo was conducive to our way of living: we'd be perfectly happy to stay inside the box – not that it'd be a box anymore. But beyond that, we can make the following statements:

> If we were all minimalists instead of conspicuous consumers, there would be less demand on the world's resources and we'd have a smaller, less berserk economy. We'd be less likely to harm the only planet we'll ever have, and the super-rich would have fewer ways to exploit us.

> If we were all cottage industrialists of part-time workers instead of bullied into being full-time employees, we'd be a liberated people, able to reconnect with labour in a modest and meaningful way.

> If we all rejected the culture of 'bigger, faster, more violent', we'd create a culture of 'smaller, slower, gentler'. Our current economic, environmental and existential problems are not the result of small, slow or gentle.

I've not annexed those statements with 'therefores' because my stance is probably clear. Put your free mind to good use and decide for yourself: would these acts be ones of selfish deviance or useful dissent? If you answer in favour of the latter, we can agree that the Escapologist's position is a morally upheld one, perhaps even one that could lead to a better world.

This book has been about individual, personal actions: what we can each do to facilitate our escapes from oppressive environments. Even so, I wish that society was more compassionate, that it afforded adequate opportunity for everyone to live freely without resorting to Escapology. Is it not the task of society – perhaps the very point of it – to provide the circumstances in which everyone has the chance of a life of freedom? A life spent making independent decisions and acting upon them?

Today's society – our prevailing attitudes to work, education and consumption – does not encourage liberty, which is why we call ourselves Escapologists: we are the ones who seek to unshackle ourselves and to erupt, unscathed, from The Trap. Escapology then, is an indictment. We should not be in a situation, especially at this late point in history, in which we feel obliged to escape. We should not feel trapped. We should not have to expend our energy going against the grain when the grain could flow in a sensible direction and encourage individual liberty for all by discouraging insatiability and rewarding citizens with the funds required for basic shelter. These suggestions should not be seen as radical or Utopian but proposals for quite basic rights, a logical extension of the progress made in the twentieth century. Humans have already accomplished far greater feats than these. We've got people in outer space at this very moment; we've got museums and libraries filled with publicly accessible works of art and literature; we've discovered the elusive Higgs boson. These are testaments to human imagination, patience and will. We can instate the minor but important changes suggested above *if we want to and if we can be bothered*. Until then, there's Escapology. Where we're not strong enough to dismantle The Trap, we can be clever and daring enough to escape it.

Let's escape individually and, one day, together. If you remain unconvinced about your own powers of escape, don't worry. It's okay. Many people remain inside The Trap their whole lives and are perfectly content with it. But if it gives you any more confidence, just remember that even Harry Houdini, patron saint of Escapology, began with nothing and that his real name was *Eric*.

Come on, let's get out of here. To Freedom!

# ACKNOWLEDGEMENTS

I'd like to thank the Unbound team, especially Mathew Clayton, Isobel Frankish, Georgia Odd, Emily Shipp, Jason Cooper, Lauren Fulbright, and John Mitchinson. Just doing your job, my foot.

Thank you to David Cain, Tom Hodgkinson, Mr Money Mustache, and Jacob Lund Fisker for connecting me to your intelligent readers. Double thanks, in fact, to David for writing the foreword and thereby letting me keep things classy.

Special mention goes to Drew Gagne and George Cockcroft for being the cavalry. Thank you both.

I'm deeply grateful to Samara Leibner, Neil Scott, Landis Blair, and Tim Eyre for the lasting friendship and advice. Thank you.

Thanks to Steve Colgan for giving me a laugh just after manuscript submission day and for introducing me to the QI gang. Thanks also to the Leacock Associates for the boost of confidence around the same time.

I'd like to thank the subscribers themselves for their generosity and patience, the fine people who responded to my surveys, the people whose ideas and lives I've mentioned in the book, my parents, sister and in-laws, and everyone who has read or contributed to *New Escapologist* over the years. I'm grateful. Thank you.

# SUBSCRIBERS

Unbound is a new kind of publishing house. Our books are funded directly by readers. This was a very popular idea during the late eighteenth and early nineteenth centuries. Now we have revived it for the internet age. It allows authors to write the books they really want to write and readers to support the writing they would most like to see published. The names listed below are of readers who have pledged their support and made this book happen. If you'd like to join them, visit: www.unbound.co.uk.

Asmah Abdul-Hamid
Brian Abernathy
Simon Adams
Dean Allen
Mugur Ardelean
Paul Arman
Christine Asbury
Nesher Asner
Lais Atilano
Kerri Augenstein
Dr. Awesome
Derren Ball
Jonathan Bank
Duncan Bannister
Michelle Barber
Jason Barnes
James Barrett
Lucy Baxter
Claire Bell

James Berry
Aaron Bishop
Sean Blacknell
Landis Blair
Tim Blanchard
Carol Blumenthal
Tom Boardman
Forlorn Boater
Kurt Bodden
Ellie Boettinger-Heasley
Steve Boggan
Dirk Bollen
Linus Boman
Piers Bonifant
Bill Bonwitt
Jaime Martínez Bowness
Nick Brodin
Craig Brooks
Marcus Brownlow

Gareth Buchaillard-Davies

Curt Buckley

Christine Bull

Anthony Bunge

Andrea Burden

Jeremy Burke

Ken Burt

Chris Bush

Marcus Butcher

John Bye

Ryan C

David Cain

John Caley

Martin Campbell

Xander Cansell

Mannix Carney

John Carnwath

Dominic Carolan

Barry Carpenter

Brenden Carpenter

Andrew Catlin

Matt Caulfield

Dominic Cave

Sean Cearley

Reggie Chamberlain-King

Jack Cheng

Georgina Churchlow

Stevyn Colgan

Mhari Colvin

David Conroy

KG Cooke

Sophie Cooper

Jeff Cornett

Jean-François Cornu

Georgia Corrick

Jessie Costin

David Cousin

John Crawford

Jez Creek

Jonathan Crook

Christy Cui

Hannah Cullen

Jenny Curren

Andrew Curry

Tom Curtis

Cornelia Daheim

Dalana Dailey

Catherine Daly

Laird of Darkness

Brian Davidson

Carl Davis

Collin Davis

Paul Davis

Nick Dawbarn

Fons de Leeuw

Jude Deeks

Sean Derbyshire

John Dexter

Terri-Jane Dow

Rachael Dowling

James Drayson

Michael Duffy

Alison Duncan

Stephen Dunkley

Anne Dye

Michelle Edwards

Scott Elliott-Brand

Charlotte Endersby

Scott Eng
Catherine Enright
Erin Erin
Kate Evans
Timothy Eyre
Sue Farthing
Paul Faux
Aimee Finn
Barry Douglas Fisher
Kim Fitzpatrick
Cait Flanders
Christopher A Forbis
Charles Forness
Clare Fowler
Rhys Fowler
Isobel Frankish
Beverly Frans
Jamie Fraser
Malene Fregil
Alan Fricker
Robert Friswell
Ian Furbank
Rich Gain
Alannah Gale
Caitlin Galer-Unti
Daniel Gallagher
Richard Paul Gamblin
Mark Garner
Marcos Gaser
Carl Gaywood
Tim Gibbs
Jo Gibson
Jessica Gioia
Frans Goddijn

Daniel Godsil
Jenny Goldsmith
Johan Gonzalez
Kevin Goodall
Nick Gordon
Emma Gorman
Jo Goudie
David Gould
Martin Greaney
Sean Greig
Roger Gronstad
Daniel Gutiérrez
William Hackett-Jones
Rustan Håkansson
Stephen Hampshire
Szilveszter Hansen
Joseph Harris
Winifred Haslam
Dirk Hasselbalch
Deborah Hastings
Meg Hawkins
Dave (hedgecutter.com)
Jonathan Hill
Rebecca Hirst
Tom Hodgkinson
Glenn Hodgson
James Edward Hodkinson
Nick Holt
Eric Hosler
Jacob Howe
Alex Howell
Holly Howell
Philip Huebner
Beverley Hurren

Shayne Husbands
Liz Hutchinson
William Hutchinson
Isaac Hutson
Christine Ibbotson
Victoria Inge
Johari Ismail
Lisa Jackson
Martin Jackson
Eric Jennotte
Mark Jerzak
Marjorie Johns
David Jones
Nick Jones
Pål Karlsen
David Keck
Patric Keller
Ryan Kelley
Hilary Kemp
James Kennedy
Dan Kieran
Reece King
Magdalena Kmak
Satu Korhonen
Sabrina Korpela
Benjamin Kovco
Mary Krell
Matthias Krug
Fabian Kruse
Jan Kuhlmann
Amina Ado Kurawa
B Lacey
Michael.Lane
@findingyourfuture.co.uk

Louise Largiader
Patricia Lawlor
Cameron and Kristi Lawrence
Joy Lawrence
Ewan Lawrie
W Tom Lawrie
Alex Leibner
John A Letham
Helen Lewis
Rob Lewis
Reuben Liang
Al Limon
Jorge Limon
Eric Lindberg
Yuen H Ling
Tomas Linhart
Tom Little
Robert Loch
Kirsty Logan
Matthew Logering
Carol Long
Nick Longson
Joanne Ludlow
Dan Mac
Iain Macdonald
Catriona Mackenzie
Miss Seonaid Mackenzie-Murray
Karen Macleod
Nick MacMillan
Anna Magombe
Kerstin Maier
Kyle F. Manning
Luben Manolov
Jean Maples